Legacy of Time:
A Tale of Three Generations

This book is dedicated to:
**My Grand Parents K. Rengasamy Chettiar
- Valliammal - Kuppammal**

My Parents - K.R.Nadesan Chettiar - Neelambal

My Wife - Ranuga Devy

Datuk Dr Ganabaskaran Nadason

Message from
Tan Sri Datuk Seri Dr. S.Subramaniam

Dato Dr N Ganabaskaran is a very well known personality within the Indian Community in Malaysia. He is born into a illustrious family in JB, where his father was a renowned business man and a philanthropist.

Although a medical doctor by profession his community involvement stretches into the social, political, and cultural spheres. He was a past national President of the Malaysian Medical Association and voiced out strong views on the health service in Malaysia. He strengthened the MMA Foundation and through his strong support the Foundation was able to continue its philanthropic activities

He was a long time senior member of the Malaysian Indian Congress and was a member of its Central Working Committee. In the MIC he was a staunch supporter of the late Tan Sri Subramaniam Sinniah, and fought many political battles along with him. He had a very colourful history in the MIC during the heydays of the Subra-Samy battle. His candid views on the management of the MIC and its associated institutions like Maika Holdings earned him the wrath of the then MIC President Tun Samy Vellu and affected greatly his progress in the political arena.

Dato Dr Ganabaskaran is a outspoken person and does not hesitate to put forward his views however controversial it may be. His contributions to the Indian Community in Johor is innumerable.

Dr Ganabaskaran is a powerful orator, capable of giving rousing speeches both in Tamil and English. He has confessed to me that he is a graceful dancer. Although he does not dance in public, I am told that he dances within the confines of his room.

I'm delighted about his endeavor to pen a book about his family, a priceless legacy for future Malaysian generations, chronicling their triumphs and national journey.

TAN SRI DATUK SERI DR. S.SUBRAMANIAM
Former Minister of Health, Malaysia
Former President of Malaysian Indian Congress

Datuk Dr. N.Ganabaskaran
A Good Friend

Datuk Dr. N.G.Baskaran's father, Mr. Nadeson Chettiar, was a MIC Leader in Johore state and supported the NLFCS during the formative stage. Following that, Datuk Dr. Baskaran too became a member of NLFCS in early 80's and was very instrumental and worked closely with Dato' Ramu and Mr. M.K. Muthusamy in support of NLFCS's growth and continued as a delegate from Johore.

I have known him since 1981 and he has became a close friend. He is the "man of community" and you cannot stop him from giving his views.

I am happy that he is writing this book on him and his family, which would be a valuable record for posterity and a benefit to the future Malaysian Generations of our struggles and success in our country.

I wish him a happy and healthy future.

Thank you.

DATUK B. SAHADEVAN
Managing Director

The Unveiling Journey

Ganabaskaran, a doctor by profession and qualification traces an incredible evolving journey as if in search of an identity. Even in his early childhood like a butterfly struggling to break out he was caught in the middle of his silver screen dreams and slapped with responsibilities as the eldest male child in a very conservative extended family. Life threw him spicy challenges as a son, big brother to his siblings and cousins, a leader to his community, a politician, a lover, a husband and a father. The cocoon took its time to shed and every layer that peeled revealed the same Baskaran –, overwhelmingly loud, courageous, generous, cheerfully persuasive, willing to help and fight for justice and serve the disadvantaged. Unfortunately all these ingredients turned out to be too idealistic in the political arena where the seamier side reared its head. His determination drove him to eventually define himself. No matter what, one could differentiate the very enthusiastic bold son from his cool father, Mr Nadeson Chettiar, an admirable cultured leader and a dignified businessman of Johor.

Born in a spice shop, Baskaran grew as if the colours and the pungent tastes of the herbs and spices groomed him to be notoriously conspicuous and in desperate search of elusive freedom. Fortunately, his family tradition and more importantly his mother, laced him well with affection, love, gratitude, respect and loyalty to his prestigious extended family till today.I must say his beautiful wife Renuga, lends her intelligence, elegance and calm to balance their life. He proudly and gratefully enlists an unwielding number of friends ranging from the very ordinary to the rich, famous and even royal not leaving out movie stars who have all influenced his life one way or another. Hats off to Baskaran's memory of people, events, dates and moments in his life!

He has told his story with no inhibitions, right from his heart as he shares his adventures of joy and sorrow, bitterness and sweetness, surprises and challenges with his solutions and resolutions.

When I read his story I could see Baskaran with a microphone tightly clutched in his hand, speaking animatedly, in volumes, without punctuations for he believes they only deter his flow!

I wish him all the best to continue his interesting journey with the best of health and happiness.

God bless.

GIRIJAH BALAKRISHNAN

17.09.22

A Journey of Loyalty:
Remembering Nadesan SAR - A Great Soul

Late Mr. K.R. Nadesan Chettiar @ Tarzin, whom I affectionately call 'SAR' despite others calling him Chief has been a die-hard supporter & ladder to many of his friends with little thought to have a early plan for himself.

Being born and brought up in Johor Bahru, I have heard, known and seen him living like a 'Chit Arasar' in the southern region of Peninsular Malaysia.

Our close relationship until his untimely death, started early 1973 where I was approached a persuaded with incentives to unseat Nadesan SAR from the post of Chairman MIC Johor Bahru Branch.

My eye to eye meet with this great man, arranged by one Mr. R. P Govindasamy proved my persuaders wrong, when I saw and could feel the sincerity in him to assist the Indian Community by and large, which instantly prompted me and my supporters to join hands rather than to oppose.

His magnanimous character was seen when he agreed to transfer Govt. Land allotted to his MIC Johor Bahru Branch to the Johor State MIC, which subsequently paved way to then the MIC President, Tan Sri V. Manickavasagam to build a 6 +1 storey impressive building in Jalan Segget, Johor Bahru.

All said and done, my closeness to the family continued being associated with his son Datuk. Dr. NG Baskaran, during his political challengers more so being in the same team, and not forgetting Nadesan SAR's beloved wife Mdm. Neelambal Nadesan another Great Soul.

Despite the up's and down, never or ever did it cross my mind that it was a wrong decision I made to support Nadesan SAR.

DATUK KRISHNAN KUNJAN PJN, PIS, AMN
Johor Bahru

Salutations to a Life Well-Lived:
A Tribute to Datuk Dr. Ganabaskaran's Autobiography

- DATO' DR. NOORUL AMEEN MOHAMED ISHACK
Founder & Executive Chairman, Qualitas Health Group

I would like to thank Datuk Dr Ganabaskaran for having thought of me to pen a few words for his Autobiography he has written and to be published soon. I briefly went through the draft he forwarded to me, and I am amazed that he had led such a colorful life and had ventured into so many facets of life and with great success with most of them.

I have heard of him during my early years as a practicing physician but did not have the opportunity to know him personally till the year 2000. We launched Qualitas Medical group in the year 1997 and had been identifying suitable doctors and clinics to join our organization. Datuk Dr Baskaran was the first doctor from Johor who agreed to join us and subsequently was instrumental in growing our network in the Johore region. He was and still is a great advocate of our business model. To date he continues to encourage us and grow the business and constantly advises us to also to diversify our offerings.

His Mentor and Father Mr Nadeson Chettiar was involved in the same business as my father was involved in Taiping and by virtue of that, they had known each other. As we grew closer, we realized that we had more common friends from all walks of life. I got to know his family, his wife and children and two of his children Namely Miss Tulasi Baskaran based in Sydney and Mr Vinod/Nadesh are very close to me. Tulasi is someone who takes care of me when I am in Sydney and Vinod is my Family Attorney. Dr Ashwini, the eldest daughter worked with us for a couple of years before she migrated to Perth.

I am glad he decided to write this book because it gives a great insight to the younger generation, what the previous generation went through and what price people pay to succeed in life. The other important lesson is unlike the current generation who are mostly self-centered and obsessed with so called work life balance, his journey shows how he spends time for religious, social, professional and personal causes and lived a full life.

In all his achievements the thing that stand out for me is how successfully he educated all his three children to be successful professionals and good human beings to add glory to him and his wife.

I wish him great success and God bless.

Unveiling the Tapestry of Three Generations:
A Biographical Prelude

It has taken me more than 5 years to write this book of my 3 generations.

What started off as a simple task developed into a mammoth task!!!

Despite the help I received from my family, relatives and friends especially Mrs.Girija Balakrishnan, (more than a sister to me) and my energetic printer Maran, I had to face certain uneventful turn of events in completing my book on time!!

When I was the President of Malaysian Medical Association from 2019 to 2020, the dreadful Covid 19 pandemic struck the world making it very difficult for all of us to meet anyone and in my case, my printer for more than 2 years!

When I was all geared up to complete my book sometime in early February 2021, I was struck by a very serious infection of the lungs called Medically Resistant Staphyloccus Aureus (MRSA) which resulted in me being hospitalised for more than 2 months and subsequently had to undergo rehabilitation for more than 6 months till October 2021!

When I finally decided to resume my writing in early January 2022, I had to set aside my writing as I had to Organise as the Organising Chairman, a major hybrid Healthy Ageing Seminar and Conference in March 2022 in Penang on behalf of the Malaysian Healthy Ageing Society!

While all these events were delaying the completion of my book, several other unfortunate events took place during the course of the last 5 years.

I lost 3 of my remaining paternal uncles and an aunty (from both of our two families) in Malaysia and India.

In July 2022, my friend and political mentor of many years Tan Sri S.Subramaniam who had been bed ridden for several years passed away.

Just 2 months of his passing away,, another political stalwart Tun Samyvelu with whom many of us were involved in our political struggle passed away suddenly in September 2022!!

The passing away of these two political giants has certainly left a void in the political circle especially in the Indian Community!!!

I am geared again to complete my book with the sponsorship from Johor Indian Education Fund and expect it to be released in February 2023.

All proceeds from the sale of my books minus the cost will be distributed to the Johor Indian Education Fund and other worthwhile education Funds in the country.

I sincerely hope it would receive the support from the youth, my friends and especially those who have been associated with me and my family for the last 100 years of our lives in this country!!

My sincere gratitude to Madam Girija Balakrishnan for her kindness and help in correcting and amending my book and to Mr.Maran of Interfocus for his patience and help in the completion of my book.

This book may not be not be in the same category as some of the biographies written by renowned authors and personalities but I am confident it would trurly reflect the struggles, tribulations, success and failures of a family of 3 generations that immigrated to this country from India for a better life!!

Happy reading!

DR. N.G.BASKARAN

Contents

My Late grandfather Rengasamy Chettiar who started it all in Malaya

Roots - The Legend

From Kalathur to Johore Baru

When life pushes you into a tight corner and you have the spirit to extricate yourself to strive for your goal, you discover the secrets to success. It is simply the result of preparation, hard work and learning from failure. You leave deep footprints of your achievements for your generations to follow.

I believe my grandfather and my father have handed down to us valuable lessons. I look up to my grandfather as a legend and my father a role model and the hero of my life.

Grandfather Late Rengasamy Chettiar with his wives - Late Madam Valliammal & Late Madam Kuppammal

Three Generations: Late K. Rengasamy Chettiar, Late K.R. Nadesan Chettiar, Dr. N.G. Baskaran

It has always been my dream and desire to write the biography of my family for my future generation to know the contribution of our forefathers and in particular, their values as good human beings. There have been so many good lessons and incidents over the last three generations that would be useful for my children and grandchildren.

It all started with my grandfather Rengasamy Chettiar, who left the shores of his native India in search of a better life in Malaya then under the

mighty British Empire. The word 'Chettiar' denotes the caste that he belonged to from the many castes that existed in India then and still do! Chettiars were basically money lenders and traders who were renowned for their business activities at home and in markets overseas especially in Southeast Asia.

My grandfather hailed from a poor farmer's family. He had a vision and a dream that gave him the strength to leave his tiny village Kalathur, about 100 kilometres away from Madras City, the capital of Madras State in India. He did not inform anyone, not even his father Kanapathy, my great grandfather. My grandfather was only 16 years then and it was in the year 1912. What hardship he went through in Malaya during those early days only God knows! But we heard that he worked tirelessly in plantations and railroads in the various parts of Malaya and finally settled down in Johor Bahru where he began working as a supervisor for the Public Works Department.

In 1926, he fell in love and married a petite, young lady called Valliammal. My grandmother hailed from Palagadu, a border town between the states of Tamil Nadu and Kerala now, but then from the undivided Madras State. Her father Manickam Mudaliar (Mudaliar being another one of those castes!!) had also come to Malaya as a labourer with his whole family. Intercast and love marriages among the Hindus were a taboo and rare those days. My grandparents had sort of created history with their marriage!

32, Jalan Segget Johor Bahru, where it all started for my late grandfather K.Rengasamy Chettiar when in 1932, he bought over a provision shop from one late Mr.Ghani who was returning back to India and renamed it as Rengasamy Chettiar & Sons. The business folded in 1969 due to difficult times. It was occupied by a tenant who was operating an Indian Restaurant called Thanusha till 2022.

Bus station next to Jalan Wong Ah Fook - 1950

Old Central Market at River Bank of
Sungai Segget 1955

She married my grandfather, who was not only a dashing and handsome young man but a very hardworking person too. Prior to moving to Johor Bahru, my grandparents stayed in a small town called Sedenak, some 30 kilometers away where their first child, Nadesan, my father, was born on 1st July 1927.

My grandfather moved his family to Johor Bahru in 1928 and was employed in the Public Works Department as a supervisor overseeing workers. My grandmother, an enterprising lady, had her own little income selling milk and other food products to her neighbours and friends.

Around 1931, impressed with my grandfather's honesty, a shopkeeper who was on the verge of going back to India for good had offered to sell him his thriving provision business. It was located at 32, Segget Street, one of the main streets of Johor Bahru. My grandfather knew this was a big break that he was waiting for in his life, but unfortunately he did not have the money except the little savings that he had. Apparently he had come home and lamented to my grandmother about the good opportunity and his inability to buy the business. On hearing this, my grandmother offered him a bundle of crushed notes she had saved and a boxful of her jewellery that she gladly gave her husband to fulfil his dream. My grandfather was dumbfounded. He was humbled with gratitude to his saviour, my grandmother.

This was the beginning of a business empire that would stretch for the next 50 years. Within the next 3 years, my grandfather had set up another spice business at No. 3, Wong Ah Fook Street, the main street in Johor Bahru. It was managed by my enterprising grandmother who also made it a home. While my grandfather was actively involved in his business, my dad seemed active too but for all

the wrong reasons!! He was never interested in his studies from young except playing truant with his friends. Despite the scoldings and beatings he did not change much to the chagrin and exasperation of my grandfather. One day in a fit of anger, he bundled him in a sack and threw him into the foul smelling Segget River in front of his shop in Wong Ah Fook Street. It was the screams and shouts from my grandmother that alerted the workers to jump into the river to save him! Who would have imagined then, that this little brat would one day become a leading entrepreneur, philanthropist and one of the most liked popular citizens of the country?

Despite this incident, there was no change in my father's habits and behaviour, compelling my grandfather to contemplate sending him to India. It was then regarded a training ground for all young men to learn the realities and hardships of life!

Having seen more than success in business, my grandfather wanted to return to India to renew his ties with his family. His family was delighted with his success story but wanted him to come back to his roots in India. The best way to do it at that time was to get him married again to one of his own relatives. Despite the fact they were aware he was already married and had children in Malaya,

Grandfather's tomb in Kezh Athivakkam Village

they convinced him. While he may have resisted in the beginning, the constant cajoling of his relatives made him marry the second time to Kuppammal without informing his first wife and not realizing the consequences of this marriage! After his successful second marriage, he returned to Malaya but never found the courage to inform his first wife. He kept it a secret as long as he could. One day, in 1936, one of the letters written by his second wife fell into the hands of his first wife!! Imagine what my grandmother did to him! She battered him till he begged for her forgiveness. What she did after that was unbelievable! She made arrangements for her rival, Kuppammal, to join them in Malaya. My grandfather was the happiest man in town with both his wives living together with him!

The First Generation

Father Late Nadesan Chettiar and
Mother Madam Neelambal Wedding Photo - 1948

My grandfather's beatings and rantings did not change my father. Exasperated, he decided to send my father to India in 1938, which he thought would be the best training ground for his son to learn the hardships of life to turn him into a responsible young man!! It turned out to be a fallacy! Despite being sent to India for correction, my father refused to change and continued with his wayward ways, even to the extent of buying a lame horse and moving from village to village with his friends. With money coming from Malaya his uncles did not bother to correct him and allowed him to continue with his gallivanting ways till the World War II broke out in 1941. Now, money from Malaya stopped coming!! Suddenly his uncles not recieving any money from Malaya started treating my father indifferently to the extent of abusing and beating him. Eventually he ran away from them and joined the Indian Army as a cook. This was the turning point in my father's life.

My uncle and the only brother of my father late Mr. Kandasamy Chettiar (Malaysian side) - Mrs. Chandra and his childrens Uma, Late Muthukumar, Dato Mohan, Rengasamy and Viji

I believe hardships often prepare ordinary people for an extraordinary destiny.

Father turned out to be a chef with great culinary skills! During the five years he was in the army he had lost contact with his family in Malaya, as war was still raging on. His family had given up on him thinking that he was dead and my grandmother constantly harassed my grandfather, as it was his fault for having sent him to India in the first place and for not trying hard enough to find her first born son!!

The war ended in 1945 and my grandparents were pleasantly surprised when they received a letter from their long lost son, informing them that he was alive and that he wanted to return home to Malaya. Travel arrangements were made and my father arrived in Malaya in 1946 much to the delight of his parents, especially my grandfather. He recognized a reformed son and a potential successor! My father had displayed his first business talent by bringing with him textiles especially Khadi clothes (immensely popular during Ghandi's Independence movement in India.) to sell in Malaya where there were several thousands of Indian nationals who were employed then.

Thus began my father's business career.

My father, who had no formal education except primary school in Tamil, realized he needed to equip himself with English and Malay if he wanted to succeed in business ventures. So he began his private tuition in Malay and English. My grandfather realized that his son had truly reformed and it was time to get him married though he was only twenty-one. It was a common practice among the Indians in those days to get their children married very young. It was a norm to find brides and bridegrooms in India. At that time, Indians in Malaya maintained their connections and loyalty with India - their motherland. There was a special emphasis to make their sons more responsible and pursue a decent career so they were able to have a

Wedding reception held by my late father in honor of Mr. R. Balakrishnan and Girija in Johor Bharu. attended by Thamizhavel G. Sarangabani, Singapore Shanugam Chettiar, Singapore Astrologer Rajamanikam, Ramakrishnan Sinniah Pillay, Johor Bharu

My father paying his respects to the Late Sultan of Johor DYMM Sultan Ismail at a function.

My father receiving first Prime Minister of Malaysia Tengku Abdul Rahman on his official visit to Johor Bharu

family of their own and be independent. The men were regarded as providers and the women, home makers including babies!

My second grandmother Kuppammal, who, after spending nearly ten years in Malaya and after having three children decided to move back to India. She was given the task of searching for a suitable bride in India for her stepson, my father. Thus began the search for a bride for my father. Love marriages were very rare those days. The criteria of a good husband or a bride was judged from the background of their families and the recommendations of the relatives concerned. It was all very practical. Looks did not matter but dowry systems was very much prevalent among the Indians. My grandfather who himself hailed from a poor and simple family had made it clear to his wife that his future daughter in law had to be a simpleton with no dowry at all!

With that in mind, the search began for a bride for my father. After a long search and having viewed several potential brides, the search ended in a village called Marakkadai, near Tiruvarur in Tanjore District, where they found this young bride of 13 years old called Neelambal!! Age was never a problem then and it was not a crime to marry someone very young. Essentially many men were cradle snatchers then! My father returned to India when they identified the bride they desired. Only for the second time for his wedding which was solemnized in 1948 to a young bride who was

hardly mature! She was brought back to Malaya to take on a housewife's role. She dutifully did that for 27 years. In the process, she became an excellent cook, a great mother for 6 children and a tolerant wife to my father who became so embroiled with public and political life in the second part of his career.

Having confidence in my father's ability, my grandfather gave him more responsibilities and travelled frequently to India, his beloved motherland, to buy properties and to procreate with his second wife. Not only did he have six children with his first wife in Malaya, he was unbiased in giving his second wife 8 children in India. My grandfather was not only busy building his business empire, he was also busy building a large family, which was the norm in those days. My grandfather was a conservative and a simple businessman with simple ideas. With his son assisting him, his businesses flourished well. He brought in more relatives from his village to help manage his expanding business. My grandfather was really a very contented man as he had more than achieved what he set out to do.

Having succeeded and fulfilled his dream in Malaya, his intention was to acquire enough wealth in India and to settle down comfortably in retirement. He achieved this by acquiring more than 150 acres of agricultural land in Keelathivakkam village, just opposite Kalathur village from where he began his life. He built a palatial bungalow and became the

Old Thandayuthabani Temple, in Johor Bharu - Built in 1920 where my late grandfather was president for 2 years and my late father was 17 years and followed by me from 1979 to 2004.

K.R. Nadesan Chettiar with P. Ramlee and L. Krishnan from Malay Filem Production Ltd. Singapore

This 90 years old pre-war building has been converted into an Indian dining outlet – Chakra Restaurant since 2006. Sultan of Johor Al-marhum Sultan Iskandar Alhaj was our regular guest. Before it became a restaurant politicians, businessmen, expatriates, foreign tourists and Singaporeans were our guests. Among them were legendary Tamil silver screen actor, the late Sivaji Ganesan, Famous Indian Actress Padmini, Famous Actor A.Nageswara Rao, poet Kannadasan and Singer Seerkazhi Govindarajan. The four rooms are named after Sivaji Ganesan, Padmini, Kannadasan and Seerkazhi in remembrance of their visits to the house.

most respected gentleman in his village till he died of diabetic complications in 1964. He was the only one who was privileged to have a tomb built in his own land within the village boundaries permitted by the village 'Panchayat' to this day.

My grandfather, though a caring and loving person, had very little interaction with his children or grandchildren, as was common among the Asian families of those days. The man of the house was boss and he only spoke to other males. His wife and children were left together and children only approached their mother for certain decisions or daily issues. Mother would bring up matters to father if big decisions had to be made. So grandfather was not casual with us and neither did he come to live with us. When my father bought his first bungalow at Jalan Yusof Taha in 1957, he readily blessed him.

Grandfather lived in his old residence at Jalan Ah Fook among the spice grinding machines!! He used to visit us regularly with fruits and goodies. I believe he had a special liking for my mother as his eldest daughter in law and the fact that she was an excellent cook. He was not a great eater and maintained his body well.

I remember my grandfather fondly and will always admire him for having come to Malaya and worked so hard to fulfil his dream.

To me, my grandfather will always be the doyen of our family and my legend.

The other doyen of our family, my grandmother Valliammal, lived with us and my uncle Kandasamy till she passed away in 1979 just before the birth of my first born Ashwini. She truly imbibes the qualities and greatness of a lady who stood by her husband in achieving his dream and experiencing success jointly!

Tamil Nadu Former Chief Minister Late Kamaraj visiting Johor Bharu 1962 and meeting with the Johor Indian Chamber of Commerce led by Late Datuk Abdul Majid, the President and my father who was the secretary then.

Photo taken on Deepavali Day 1960
Sarojini, Lakshmi, Shanmugam, Venugopal, Myself and on the lap of my mother is
my youngest brother Arumugam

My Hero

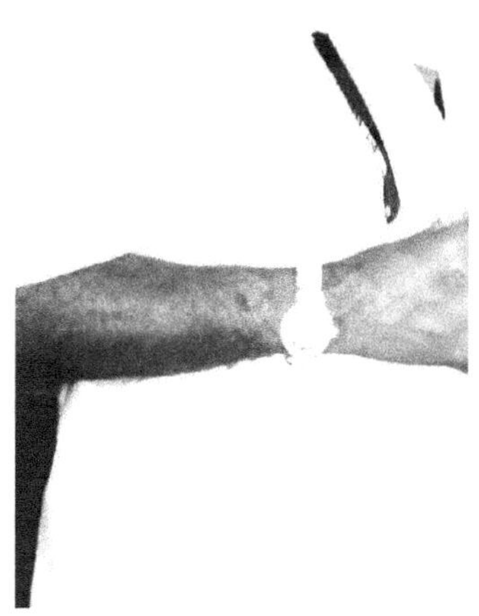

My father had his own dreams. He realized Malaya had great business potential and it was a country he wanted to be in, unlike his father. His dreams were much bigger and his plans much grander. He wanted to venture into different businesses and create a business empire of his own. He knew the time was right and for the next ten years he worked tirelessly and diligently. His family was involved in retail household provision business that he managed to turn into a major wholesale business supplying packed food products throughout Malaya. It soon became the forerunner to many others.

He also discovered the great potential in property and real estate business and started acquiring properties in various places including a 100 acre-estate that was named after me as Baskar estate. This was later to become the famous Taman Tun Aminah in Scudai, after he sold the property in the late 60s. The other property he acquired was a large tract of land in the famous Lido Beach (where Danga Baby is now). Subsequently, he sold it back to the Government against good advice to complete

My father receiving the Late Sultan of Johor DYMM Sultan Iskandar who was visiting The Sri Subramaniam Temple in Masai.

his dream housing project Taman Majidee Park. To describe his business acumen would be too big a list but nevertheless he truly had the Midas touch. Everything he touched became gold including his wholesale business that he established in Market Street in Singapore in 1957. All was well until he met with his first major business blow in 1959!!

Having resided for most of his life with his family at our business premises at 3, Wong Ah Fook, amidst the spice grinding machines, he acquired a bungalow at 1, Jalan Yusof Taha in 1957 a memorable home graced by many great personalities from all over Malaya and overseas. My grandfather stayed shy of public life except for being the President of Thendayuthapani Temple

and a trustee of the Mariamman temple. Both the temples were in Johor Bahru where everything began for him. For the next three generations, members of my family succeeded as Presidents of Thendayuthapani Temple.

My father became the President of the Thendayuthapani temple in 1958 following his father's footsteps and continued for the next seventeen years. I then became the President in 1979 and continued till 2004 after completing the consecration. of the new temple in 1999.

My father, while building his business empire became more and more prominent. He was slowly drawn into public and political life. He became the first president of The Tamil Association of Johor Bahru, in the early 50's and continued till his death in 1975, when it became defunct. I revived the association in 1977 and became the second President till 1980 making my own entry into public life.

In 1958, he became the Secretary of the Johor Indian Chamber of Commerce and subsequently its President for many years till his death. As the secretary of the Johor Indian Chamber of Commerce he was appointed to the Johor State Legislative Assembly in 1959. He was also Founder and President of Johore Ghandian Society formed in the 60's to propagate Ghandian Ideals and played his role as President till his death. The state government through the efforts of my father even gave a prominent piece of land to the society in

Sivaji greeting my grandmother Madam Valliammal with me standing in between (1961)

Johor Bahru to build a Ghandian hall that has never been fulfilled to date!! He was drawn into politics and became the Chairman of the Johor Bahru MIC branch in 1960 getting deeper and deeper into public and political life that propelled him into State and National levels. This marked the beginning of his downfall in business.

In 1959, when he was at the height of his business career, he received his first blow. His wholesale food business at Market Street in Singapore was thriving under a supposedly trustworthy manager called Panchacharam who managed the business while my father residing in Johor Bahru was travelling on a daily basis to Singapore to oversee the collection and accounts. One fine day, Panchacharam absconded to India with a weekend collection of more than 50,000 Singapore dollars in hand worth a million Singapore dollars today. Luckily for my father,

The family of late singer Seerkazhi Govindarajan during his first visit to Malaya in 1961 to perform in concerts throughout Malaya which were organised by my father.

Panchacharam had remitted the money through the black money market or famously known as the Hawala market. The money in India was handled by an Indian Muslim businessman and money changer who was aware that Panchacharam was working for my father. Suspicious of his sudden wealth, the money changer contacted my father and informed him about the large sum that Panchacharam had remitted. My father flew to India to recover his money. He was able to recover the money but only over a period of time. One can imagine what my dad would have done to Panchacharam if he saw him again. Apparently, Panchcharam returned to seek father's forgiveness after having committed such a wilful crime. Instead of punishing him, my father apparently forgave him and in fact bought him his return flight ticket to Singapore. Unbelievable! But that was my father!! That was the first lesson my father learnt to trust his earnings with someone else. Unfortunately, very soon he learnt more about how trust in his political and public life could turn vile and strike him.

My father was a very generous soul and anyone who came to him for help never left empty handed. One of his many passions was to entertain visitors and friends with lunches and dinners much to the agony of my mother who spent most of her time in the kitchen for the 27 years she was married to him! My mother is an excellent cook and even till today she enjoys cooking some of her best dishes. Her signature dish is fish head curry for our family and friends. We were one of the most prominent Indian families in town and with my father in social and political activities also had a passion for hospitality. It is typically Indian tradition to serve food to anyone who visits your home. But, perhaps my father was too enthusistic and proud of his wife's cuisines. It was normal to have as many as 20 to 50 guests at any point of time for lunches and dinners in my house. My house had heavy traffic of visitors and guests who came from all over the country and overseas especially India. My mother takes pride in cooking her own dishes without the help of any maids or helpers even till today.

In 1961, my father's younger brother Kandasamy married Chandra from India and brought his wife home. But as fate would have it she too joined my mother in cooking for the guests! It must have been a nightmare for both my mother and my aunty because the spread of dishes was always elaborate and my father very often would give mother very short notice to prepare the food. The chefs never complained and people enjoyed coming to our house for these tasty meals. Many of these tales

My Father with Late R.Balakrishnan, Late Venkadesan and other friends in chennai - 1973

were related to me in my subsequent years when I became involved in public life. The guests they said ranged from the ordinary man on the street to famous politicians, actors, actresses, poets, writers and speakers.

Some of the more prominent guests who have been entertained in our house were:

- Tun V.T. Sambanthan the 5th President and the first Malaysian Indian Minister
- Dato V. Manickavasagam the 6th MIC President and Minister.
- Mr. C. Subramaniam Former Finance Minister of India.
- Mr. Murasoli Maran, Nephew of Mr. M. Karunanidhi, former Chief Minister of Tamil Nadu and Federal Minister
- Tamizhavel Sarangapany from Singapore

My father's very close friend Vallal Rengasami Pillay

Third Prime Minister of Malaysia the late Tun Hussein Onn who was greeted by my father who was his close friend in Johor Bharu when he assumed the position of Deputy Prime Minister in 1975

South Indian Actors

- Sivaji Ganesan leading actor of Tamil Nadu.
- Nageswara Rao from Andhra Pradesh
- Kavignar Kannadasan Tamil poet/lyric writer
- Padmini and Ragini Renowed Indian actresses
- Mathuram wife of NS Krishnan Leading comedian of the silver screen.
- Seerkazhi S, Govindarajan, famous movie and classical singer
- Ma Po Sivagnanam from Tamil Nadu, a geat writer and orator

Local stalwarts in Politics and Public Service:

- Datuk K Pathmanaban Deputy Minister
- Dato S.Subramaniam Deputy Minister
- Mr R Balakrisnan Head of Indian Service Radio Malaysia
- Vallal Rengasamy Pillai Philanthropist Penang

Most or almost all of the above personalities have since passed away. (Bless their souls)

My father, being a simple person, developed a close rapport with people from all walks of life including the Malay and Chinese communities. He was particularly close with Chief Ministers of Johor and Malaysia's third Prime Minister, Tun Hussein Onn, who was the Parliament member for Johor Baru for many years.

In 1980, when I was serving as a medical officer in Mersing for a short while, I had the privilege to meet the Late Tun Hussein Onn who was visiting Mersing with his family. I went up and introduced myself when he was having lunch with his family. He made me sit next to him to have lunch with his family. As he related the wonderful friendship he had with my late father I could see he remembered him fondly. That was one of the most emotional moments in my life and made me realize how my late father had created special bonds with people and the impact he had created in their minds with his sincere friendship. That meeting with Tun Hussein Onn was one of my best moments in my life. In my subsequent years, in public and political life, I met several people who had known my father and all of them told me without exception what a genuine and good man he was. No amount of wealth could generate the amount of goodwill my father had left us!

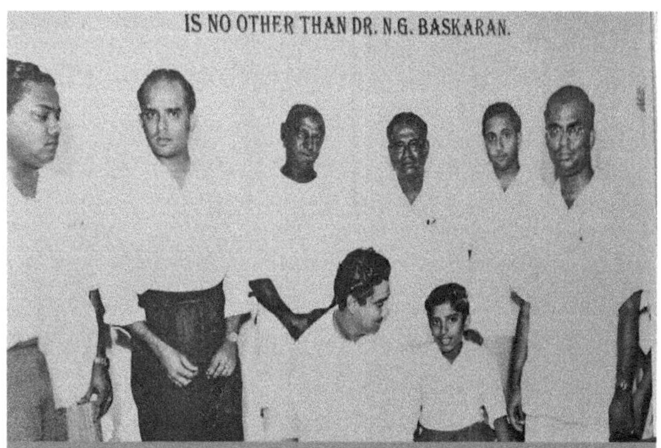

Together with my favourite actor the Most Famous South Indian Actor Late Nadigar Thilagam Sivaji Ganesan who visited my home in 1961 after receiving the best actor Award in Afro-Asian Film Festival

When I was young, I was not able to appreciate the good qualities of my father as I was too young and my father was never close to us. He was always found in the company of his friends. This was very typical of most Asian families during those days. But nevertheless as I grew older, I realized I did not need any hero or mentor other than my father as he had shown all those great qualities that makes a good human being.

My father was kind, generous; warm hearted and an atypical politician as he was honest and sincere to all the leaders and friends he cared for. Unfortunately, all his friends whom he had supported during the course of his political career were not equally reciprocal!

Father with MIC fifth president Tun Sambanthan at a reception held in his honour in Johor Bharu

Snakes and ladders in politics

What started as a casual foray into political and public life for my father finally turned out to be his downfall. He was never cut out to be a politician, as he was not an opportunist and never had the killing instinct of a politician. In 1967, when he was very popular as Vice Chairman of the Johor Malaysian Indian Congress, he was unanimously proposed to take over as the State Chairman at the State Delegates Meeting. He declined, claiming he was a businessman and not a politician and in the process gave way to the then treasurer of the state and his good friend Mr. G. Pasamanickam. Later Mr Pasamanickam became a Datuk and Tan Sri, titles that are awarded by the Sultans of the various Malaysia states and by the King for services rendered to the states and the nation. He was keen to become the next State Chairman and hence he took on the then incumbent and State Assemblyman, Mr. Kumaran (deceased now) and defeated him to become the State Chairman.

My father had secured a promise from Mr. Pasamanickam prior to the elections, to allow Mr. Kumaran, the incumbent State Assemblyman to re-contest in the General Election due in 1969, whatever the outcome of the Chairman's contest was. Mr. Pasamanickam gladly agreed to my father's proposal! Having been elected as the State Chairman, Mr. Pasamanickam began planning and charting a firm career in politics. He was a shrewd politician and a great planner that eventually lead him to be active in politics

Father with MIC sixth president Tan Sri Manickavasagam at a reception held in his honour in Johor Bharu

for more than 40 years especially in Johor and in national politics!

In 1969, prior to the General Elections, there was an explicit understanding between my father, Mr. Pasamanickam and Mr. Kumaran that the State MIC would negotiate for three seats in the forthcoming elections from the then ruling coalition the Alliance party. The areas were Masai, Muar and the existing Batu Anam constituencies respectively for the three of them if they were able to secure the seats from the Alliance leadership failing which the sole assembly seat of Batu Anam would be given to the incumbent Mr. Kumaran for another term. The state leadership was unable to secure the three seats as expected and as agreed upon,

Mr. Kumaran was nominated by the State MIC leadership to be the MIC and Alliance candidate in the forthcoming general elections. This was when Mr. Pasamanickam turned on his political wizardry. While MIC has always been touted as a party for all Malaysian Indians since its formation in 1946, divisions on the basis of race and caste had always existed in MIC and does till today. My father and Mr. Pasamanickam were Tamils from the Major ethnic group among the Malaysian Indians whereas Mr. Kumaran was a Malayalee the third largest ethnic group among the Malaysian Indians.

Mr. Pasamanickam decided to play on ethnic sensitivity as the then MIC President the late Datuk V.T. Sambanthan was a Tamil! This has been the

tradition with MIC to this day. Mr. Pasamanickam was able to convince Datuk V.T. Sambanthan who as the MIC President would be nominating candidates on behalf of MIC to the Alliance party. Mr. Pasamanickam played his racial card well and in the process had convinced Datuk Sambanthan that as the incumbent State MIC Chairman, it was important for him to have an elected position to be an effective leader.Like most politicians, he deliberately played out my father for personal gains. Despite the fact that Datuk Sambanthan had always valued my father's friendship and hospitality both as a friend and as a leader, he had to make a political decision against that of the Johor State MIC. Ignoring the understanding that existed between the three State leaders on the allocation of seats for the forthcoming general elections, Datuk Sambanthan was better convinced by Mr. Pasamanickam's supporters that Mr Pasamanickam would make a better candidate.

Tan Sri G. Pasamanickam

Mr Kumaran the incumbent assemblyman and a gentleman by nature believed the agreement between the state leaders would be honoured and that he would be the candidate for the next general elections and was thus preparing for his nomination. Much to his agony and despair, Datuk Sambanthan announced Mr. Pasamanickam as the candidate for the Batu Anam state seat in 1969. This led to complete chaos and turmoil in the Johor State MIC earning the wrath of my father. He was annoyed with Mr. Pasamanickam for not honouring the promise he had made to him and Mr. Kumaran. Having realized that he was not being nominated as a candidate Mr. Kumaran had come straight to my father and cried his heart out. Despite my father's attempts to convince Datuk Sambanthan on the decision of the State Committee and the agreement and understanding that existed between the state leaders on the allocation of seats, he failed to convince him and ended in a legal battle.

Mr. Pasamanickam having filed his nomination as a candidate came straight to meet my father in my house apparently to seek his blessings but was stopped at the entrance of my house. My father enraged told him that he should only enter his house as his old friend and not as his political friend! Despite

M.P. Kumaran

Mr. Pasamanickam's attempts to explain and pacify my father, he refused to accept Mr. Pasamanickam's 'explanation' as Mr. Pasamanickam had breached his promise to him and Mr. Kumaran. This led to a long drawn political battle for the next six years till the death of my father!

Mr. Pasamanickam won the election in Batu Anam in 1969 but my father moved swiftly to take a court injunction against Mr. Pasamanickam to prevent him from being sworn in as an assemblyman. Unfortunately, due to the racial riots that took place on May 13th 1969 immediately after the general elections, a state of emergency was declared throughout Malaysia by the Federal government and a National Operation Council was formed to manage the country thus making my father's attempt to secure an injunction against Mr. Pasamanickam's to fail.

When the emergency was lifted in 1970, Mr Pasamanickam took his oath of office as an Assemblyman in the Johor State Assembly and was subsequently appointed to the State Exco after the 1974 general election which is equivalent to a state minister by the then Chief Minister of Johor, Tan Sri Othman Sa'at, a personal friend of Pasamanickam. They both hailed from Muar town in Johor.

Though my father was persistent on pursuing the legal suit against Pasamanickam which was filed against him before the General Elections, he was personally requested by Dato Sambanthan the MIC President to withdraw the suit as the appointment of Pasamanickam to the State Assembly was very important and relevant to the Indian Community in Johor. Taking this into consideration my father withdrew the suit, thus leading the way for Pasamanickam to become a state assemblyman for the next five years. Subsequently, he won a second term in 1974. He continued as an Exco member, and as the Johor State MIC Chairman for a period of nearly 22 years which made him the longest serving MIC State Chairman to date.

Subsequently, my father's attempts to take on Pasamanickam for the MIC State Chairman's post in the party elections held in 1970, 1971, and 1972 did not materialize because by then many had crossed over to Pasamanickam's side and he himself had become politically very powerful.

MIC national politics took a turn in 1971 when Dato V. Manickavasagam the then MIC Deputy President decided to take on Dato V. Sambanthan, the MIC President for the MIC President's post. Dato V. Sambanthan had served more than 17 years as MIC President's. My father who had been close to both Dato V. Sambanthan and Dato V. Manickavasagam believed that there should be a change in this leadership. Many saw Dato V. Manickavasagam as the next MIC President much to the surprise and shock of Dato V. Sambanthan. The battle lines were drawn and many in MIC had

to decide whom to support in this crucial contest. Dato Pasamanickam like many other State MIC Chairmen decided to support Dato V. Sambanthan the incumbent, whereas my father threw his support behind Dato V. Manickavasagam for which he was suspended from the party by Dato V. Sambanthan. As the Presidential Election took an ugly turn with suspensions and expulsions of party leaders by Dato V. Sambanthan, Tun Abdul Razak the then Prime Minister and Chairman of the Alliance coalition intervened to bring peace into MIC. An accord was reached between Dato V. Sambanthan and Dato V. Manickavasagam. It was agreed that Dato V. Sambanthan would step down as MIC President in 1973 thus paving the way for Dato V. Manickavasagam to become the new President of MIC in 1973.

When Dato V. Manickavasagam became the president there was joy among his supporters, including my father and his supporters in Johor, who felt that there would be a leadership change in Johor, since Dato G. Pasamanickam had actively supported Dato V. Sambanthan in the MIC leadership struggle which did not eventually materialize. Unfortunately, much to the chagrin of my father and his supporters no leadership change took place in Johor because of the shrewd and intelligent manipulation of politics by Dato G. Pasamanickam among the top leadership of MIC and to those close to Dato V. Manickavasagam.

MIC PERAK

Game Over

My father, though appointed to MIC Central Working Committee by Dato V. Manickavasagam, never lived to see the leadership change in Johor MIC as he passed away in 1975.

My father who had sacrificed a lot for public, social and political services died under difficult circumstances! With no formal education he rose on his own merits and dedication to become one of the richest Indians in Johor. In fact, a multi-millionaire at the age of 38 years only to lose everything by the young age of 48 when he passed away in 1975. The proof of his great life was when more than 5000 people and leaders from all walks of life from throughout Malaysia attended his funeral on August 7th 1975 in Johor Bahru and gave him an emotional send off to a better world. To me, he will always remain the best father, a wonderful and philanthropic soul and most of all a great human being!! Taman Majidi, the Thendayuthapani Temple and the Gandhian society in Johor Bahru will carry his name etched in the history of Johor not forgetting the thousands of needy people and students who received timely help from him.

He walked tall among his peers both as a Malaysian and as a Malaysian Indian!! To me, my father will always remain a hero!!

He was a self made true entrepreneur especially among the Malaysian Indian community. He forayed into the Spice Industry by packaging, marketing and distributing spices throughout Malaysia, becoming the forerunner for others to follow. He went into wholesale trading, importing and marketing of essential food items in Malaysia and Singapore.

He became the first Indian in Johor to build the first housing estate called Taman Majidee in Johor Bahru comprising of more than 200 mixed housing units.

He went into active social, religious and political public life both at the State and National level in Malaysia to help the needy. He was the Chairman and President of several organizations namely The Malaysian Indian Congress, Thendayuthapani Temple, The Indian Chamber of Commerce and The Gandhian Society.

He was a great philanthropist having given away millions for various charitable institutions and to hundreds of students for their studies.

He was admired and known for his entertaining qualities and generous dinner parties.

He was a friend not only to the leaders of the country, the rich and famous, and businessmen but also to people across the strata of our society. He was a friend to Indians, the Malays and the Chinese.

He became one of the richest Indians in Johor making his first million when he was hardly 38 years and losing it all when he passed away at the young age of 48. He did not leave us much wealth or properties but he left us with good education and a lasting name, money can never buy. All of us, his six children salute him and will always cherish his memory!!

His tomb at Johor Bharu Hindu Cemetry

*With my father at
the age of 3 in 1953*

Second Generation - My Early Life

On AUGUST 4TH 1950 at 6.30 PM, I became the first born of my parents and to the joy of my grandparents who believed that I would traditionally carry on their future family name as is the norm among Asian families. There was a great celebration. As the saying goes,' Aasthikku oru magan, aasaiku oru penn' (for assets a son, for love a daughter). I was delivered by an experienced midwife, amidst the lingering smell of various spices that were milled on the ground floor of No 3 Jalan Ah Fook. Must have been such an unforgettable and tormenting experience for my young mum who was only 15 years old then!!

Imagine being born to one of the richest families in Johor Bahru at that point of time, and especially if the family acquires more properties and assets after your birth, you are quite often considered as a lucky addition to the family!! These are traditional beliefs among the Indians and possibly with other Asian families even till today! Obviously and quite luckily I fell into this category!! My family acquired a 100 acre- rubber plantation in Scudai about ten kilo meters from Johor Bahru after my birth and named it Basker Estate!! After it was sold in 1970 to a developer, it became the

famous Taman Tun Aminah. After me there were seven more siblings added to our family losing two of them to birth complications - no fault of the same experienced midwife who delivered all of us. The final count left me with two sisters Sarojini the second, Thanalakshmi the fourth and three brothers Venugopal the third, Shanmugam the fifth and Arumugam the sixth in our family. Four of us were delivered at our Wong Ah Fook residence amidst the spices and the last one in the comfort of our new bungalow at 1, Yusof Taha Street Johor Bahru after 1957.

While I am unable to recollect my past up to the age of six, I believe I had a very comfortable life and had all the traits of a normal growing child. According to my mom, who had to manage six children within a period of ten years, I was the most well-behaved child and easiest to manage!! If only I had remained that way for the rest of my life, I would have saved myself from several problems and complications that would be taking place during my life- time.

I started my primary schooling in 1957, at the famous Ngee Heng English Primary school in the afternoon after attending the Tamil Primary School at Jalan Duke in the morning. My father was a total believer in Tamil, our mother tongue and was totally committed in the propagation of the language, as he was also then the President of the Tamil Association of Johor. My only memory of that period is rushing to both the schools on foot, despite the fact that we had enough vehicles at our disposal. That was the type of upbringing we had!! I also remember having a weak bladder and often running to the toilets and quite occasionally wetting myself in the bargain and being embarrassed in front of my mum. Thank God, it was my mum, because there is no soul in the world who would understand me better!

I had to give up the Tamil school in my second year of schooling because of some government restriction and had to continue my Tamil education as home tuition. Subsequently, I was moved to the newly constructed Temenggong Abdul Rahman School to continue my school, where I first met my lifelong friends. I still have vivid memories of those days. I cannot forget all the good and bad times we experienced together and am proud to say we have remained friends to date. There are no words to describe the kind of true and meaningful friendship we developed in school and college, unlike the kind of friendship we develop during our later years when we are trying to build our career and future. The most memorable days are the formative years in school and college days!!

Temenggong Abdul Rahman School

Fifth Johor Sea Scouts - 1963

My Illustrious School Days

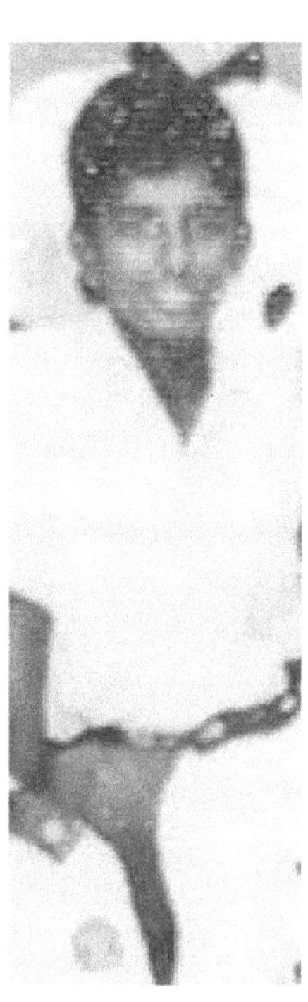

During my Primary school days, I had two sets of friends. One group consisted mainly of non Hindu, Indian friends, like Bobby Chin, Raghbir Singh (in USA now), Daniel Loh (deceased), Donald Choo Keng Kit, Lew Jan Miew, Fadzil Abdullah, Ahmad Mansor, Ibrahim Bakar, Sanusi Junid, Rosli Hussein and Zainal Abidin- a cross section of our society. They were studious and remained close friends of mine to date. The other circle of Indian friends, like Arumugam, Maniam and Manoharan from the lower income group of the society were naughty and basically not interested in studying. The only exception in this group was Jambulingam. He was a very hardworking, studious student from a middle income family who subsequently married my eldest sister Sarojini in 1977!!

I have never got over the fact that I was able to get along well with both these divergent groups in my schooldays. I believe if I ever socialised well with both these groups, it was basically lessons learnt from my father. He moved with a diversified group

of friends from the various strata of societies who were regular visitors and guests in my home. As a teenager, I picked up a few bad vices like smoking and drinking from friends like Clement D'Cruz who never made it in his studies but subsequently became a big time and colourful businessman in Johor Bahru. My extra allowance came from my father's pockets and with continuous successful pickpocketing I upgraded myself to the red ten ringgit notes!

During my secondary school days in English College (renamed as Sultan Abu Bakar College subsequently) the premier institution in Johor, I was very active in various school associations. I was the Chairman of the school library board, the Secretary of the Badminton Club, a member of the school badminton team and a member of the Boy Scouts' movement. I believe these positions moulded me as a leader to lead several organizations in the later part of my life.

During my schooldays, interaction among the various races and friends was at its best. We even acquired entrepreneurial skills as Form Four students in 1966. We decided to launch a

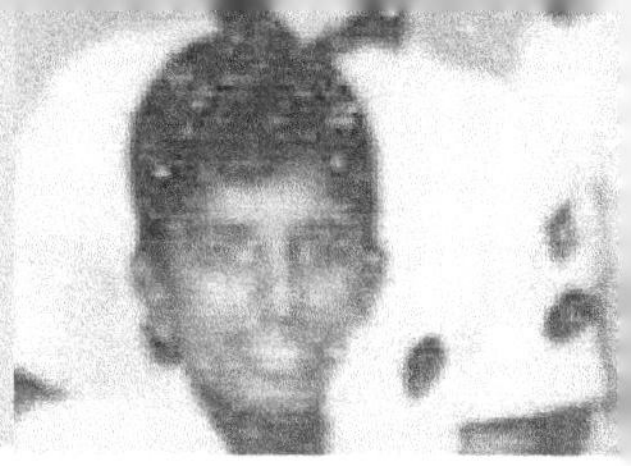

English College, Johor, Form 5 Science - 1967

class magazine of our own called 'BLEEP' with our classmates as shareholders paying 50 cents for a share and we could acquire as many shares according to our affordability. I was the business manager. The magazine turned out to be a big hit since we sold it not only in our school but in all other schools in town. The returns were handsome as all shareholders were paid a minimum of Ringgit 5 depending on their investment and that was really good for those days. My classmates and I, though from the Science stream (those from science stream were thought to be studious, nutty, snobbish and without talents!) created a musical group called Microwave 5 (comprising of my classmates Daniel, Fadzil, Bobby, me and an outside friend called Dusty) and managed to win an open talent time contest in 1967 in Johor Bahru.

My classmates even created a drama called 'Time Tunnel' for the inter school drama competition in 1967 and won the first prize!! It was hilarious and my role was the main character as a drunkard!! I travelled to the Stone Age through the time tunnel by a nutty scientist Ibrahim Bakar and assisted by Fadzil Abdullah. I meet the cavemen headed by

Daniel Loh as their leader and Roland Ng as his lovely wife. The joke was, they were the fattest classmates of ours!! The rest of our classmates acted as cavemen. It was a great drama and everyone loved it and congratulated us. We even had a few admirers from the girls' schools much to our delight and excitement!! Those were the unforgettabled days as teenagers!!

I loved both Tamil and English movies and music from young. I was particularly interested in Indian movies and music, for the love of the Tamil language and my Indian friends were all the way with me. There were four cinema theatres, Rex, Capital, Broadway and subsequently Cathey in my hometown Johor Bahru and they screened about two Tamil movies per month, per theatre, which served my purpose very well to play truant and go to for these movies with my Indian friends. Though my family was quite comfortable, I was short of money for little luxuries. My father was rather strict about pocket allowance but the occasional pickpocketing from my father's pockets helped me to fulfil my little desires!! I even ventured into Singapore to see the latest Indian movies since there were no passport requirements in those days. There were two theatres in Singapore called Diamond and Royal and they screened Tamil pictures mainly. I remember those days fondly because I was often taken to these theatres by my father between 1957 and 1961 when he had a thriving wholesale business at 48 Market Street in Singapore. I used to wait eagerly during my school holidays to be invited by my father to Singapore to oversee his business. After the routine business checks, he used to take me for lunch at one of the famous restaurants Islamic or Jubilee in Singapore. After lunch, we were off to the movies most of the time to one of the two theatres Royal or Diamond.

I have been the luckiest among my siblings. I remember with fondness the Diamond theatre for it was there that I won the first lucky prize in a draw that was conducted to celebrate the continuous run of aTamil movie called Pavamannippu in 1960 with a stellar cast headed by the famous doyen of Tamil movies Mr. Sivaji Ganesan! It was the first lucky prize I won in my life and it will always be etched in my memory. Little did I realize that I would be sitting next to the same Mr. Sivaji Ganesan and talking to him in 1961 in my house in Johor Bahru when he was invited to celebrate his winning of the

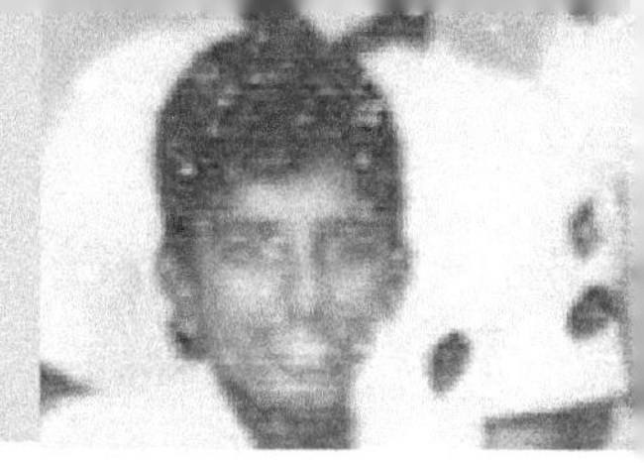

My School friends from 1959 till 1967 in Temmengong Abdul Rahman and English College Johor Bahru

best actor award in Afro-Asia for his outstanding performance as Veerapandiya Kattapomman. He depicted the first South Indian king who fought the British Empire for India's independence. It was one of the best movies ever produced by the Tamil Film Industry and to me it remains as one of the greatest moments of my life!!

Though I was given to minor vices introduced to me by my Indian friends during my formative years, I am grateful to my non Indian friends for all the strength, constructive and positive activities in life, such as studies, sports and wholesome outings. I was not a great sportsman in the Primary School Days but loved badminton and swimming and excelled in them. Badminton was my favourite sports in my secondary and college days. I was a little naughty in Primary school doing the normal pranks for which I received occasional rebukes and whipping from my disciplinary teacher Mr. Prasad, whom I became familiar with later as one of the MIC branch Chairmen in Pontian.

Despite my mischievious ways, I was quite popular among the teachers. One Miss. Sinnadurai was particularly fond of me and made me the class monitor and a school prefect giving me the opportunity to become a responsible student. I also had the greatest pleasure of the presence of Sinnadurai and her husband at the wedding of

My classmates of primary and secondary schools (Temmengong Abdul Rahman School and English College in Johor Bharu)

my eldest daughter Dr. Ashwini in 2007. Imagine being in touch with my Primary school teacher after 45 years!! Another teacher I remember quite well was Mr. Gurdial Singh who not only taught me in Primary school but subsequently in Secondary school as well. Teachers of those days taught us with much dedication, love and discipline. Their care and dedication make us remember them fondly even after 50 years. Another teacher whom I remember with respect is Mr. Ramalingam who was my tuition master. Not only was he a great teacher but a good human being who became a personal friend of my father and mine subsequently. With such dedicated and committed teachers to teach and guide us, most of my non Indian classmates made it with me to secondary school with good results in 1963.

While my primary school days were innocent and carefree days, the real learning curve began during my secondary school days!! Simple little pleasures became major pleasures on attaining the teenage status, a period when we start discovering new interests in life. Music, dancing and the desire to become friendly with female students were the needs and norms of the day. Attaining puberty came with its own problems! Innocent mind becomes invaded by unnecessary thoughts and requirements. The popularity and wealth of my father became additional factors in the development of values in my life and those of my siblings. Like my Primary school days, I also had two sets of friends during my secondary school days. One the usual intelligent and hardworking school friends

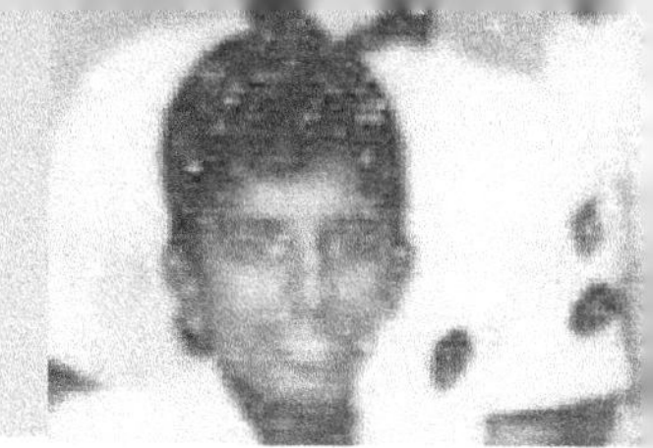

and the other my usual Indian friends not in my school. They were there with me for my movie outings and other minor vices. My classmates were not only excellent in their studies but also shone in sports and in all extracurricular activities of the school. We were lucky to have great and dedicated teachers like Mr. Gurdial Singh senior, Mr. Samuel whom we fondly refer to as Uncle Sam who was a great dancer in his own right!! Mr. P.C. Joseph (with a peculiar cough), Mr. D. Pillai, Mr. Sundaram, Mr. Perry, Mr. Wong, Mr. Maurice Khoo, Mr. Naidu, Mr. Chandra and many others. I even remember my Tamil school teachers. Mr. Anthonysamy, Mr. Athimulam, Mrs. James and my Tamil tuition teachers Mr. Doraisamy who taught me initially and Mr. Velumail who taught me till my Senior Cambridge exams.

I did Tamil as an exam subject and scored a C3 in Senior Cambridge which was a strong credit!! The teachers were not only dedicated but also played a major role in our moral upbringing!! It would be difficult to forget such wonderful human beings to whom all of us should be eternally grateful!! Many of them have left the world but they have left enough students to speak of their dedication.

We were lucky to have a Peace Corps volunteer teacher Mr. Lomax, who created the Day Camps in our school. The day camps played a pivotal role in bringing together students from the various schools in Johor Bahru (especially the female students from two of the famous schools of those days, Convent and SIGS to interact and participate in extracurricular activities during the long December school vacation. We were the first batch of students who initiated this day camp and it turned out to be a wonderful experience, creating friendship and fellowship among the various schools and students. What a time we had seeking the attention of the female students surrounding us!! We sat for our Senior Cambridge exams in 1967. The best part of the exam was I decided to sleep over my physics paper, a subject I hated most. Little did I realize that I would be taking the same paper the next year during my PUC days in India!

After our Senior Cambridge days, we, friends had to part to seek our future and fortune taking different paths but the good thing was we were in touch regularly with one another. I was even fortunate enough to invite many of my primary and secondary school classmates for my eldest daughter Dr. Ashvin's wedding in 2007!! The feeling was great!! The good fortune of having dedicated teachers paved the way to success for many of us. My ambition from young had always been to become lawyer or an actor at the least having acted with some success in our school dramas!!

Maternal Uncle Rajamanickam Chettiar on SS Rajula on
4th March 1968 on the way to India for my studies

My Journey To India

My exam results were due to come out on 5th March 1968 but my father who never really got involved in my education during the last 17 years, had made my booking to travel on 4th March 1968 on S.S. Rajula to Chennai. Perhaps he was more confident than me that his son won't let him down?? If only he knew the state of mind I was in, not having sat for the physics paper! I panicked.

All the necessary preparations including shopping were done and the day arrived for me to leave the country for the first time in my life. I did not realize that this journey was leading me to the real lesson in growing up with the many life experiences that I was to encounter in my seven years to come in India!!

I boarded SS Rajula, from Singapore the nearest port for us from Johor Bahru. I was sent off with the full entourage of my parents, family, relatives, and family friends. What an emotional send off it was!! Everyone was hugging and kissing me with tears in their eyes. The ship sailed away bearing all our dreams.

When the ship started sailing, the fear of my exam results coming out the following day gripped me. I was already sailing and there was no turning back with so much hope pinned on me by my family. Thoughts fleeted through my mind, the most important being the present financial situation of my family that was on the decline. My father never ever discussed this with his children.

The iconic SS Rajula

I checked into my cabin that I was sharing with someone I was not familiar with. I started moving around the ship making friends. That has been my nature all my life. Though I was not a drinker, I was independent now and sat around with a couple of guys to drink some beer basically to forget my worries about my exam results. The ship berthed the following day at Port Klang, our next stop and that is when I noticed several students boarding the ship.

I was having lunch when I was approached by a tall gentleman who asked me if I was Baskaran and when I acknowledged, he introduced himself as Selvaraj, the secretary of Mr. R. Balakrishnan, a close family friend who was head of the Indian Section of Radio Malaysia.

He grabbed my hand, shook it and said the most wonderful words I heard in my life. Congratulations!! You have passed with grade one in the exams!! My heart nearly stopped and I could not believe what I was hearing. He handed me a small parcel and said that it was a gift from Mr. Bala. I thanked him and after a small chat, mostly the good things about my father, he left never realising that he would become a good friend of mine in later years.

I was reeling in shock and it took me sometime to accept the fact that I had passed my exams and that too with a grade one!!

That night was celebration time, sharing my joy with my co passengers with good food and beer. This time around in joy rather than in worry.

The next day the ship arrived in Penang, our next stop. Here again, I was met by an assistant of the famous philanthropist Mr. Rengasamy Pillai, another close family friend of ours, never realising for a moment that this bond of true friendship would be continuing for the next 45 years or more with the next generation as well. I was taken to his large bungalow and given a sumptuous meal for which he was known for, I received a gift from him too, along with good advice that I should study hard, become a doctor and make my family proud.

It was back to the ship in the afternoon and I noticed this time around to a large number of students boarding. This was the final stop in Malaysia before reaching the shores of Madras that would take us another four days in the high seas. As I started mingling with my co passengers, I realised that there were few hundred students both seniors who were returning to India to continue their studies whereas we juniors had just embarked on our careers.

Normally, when the senior students meet the juniors they begin with a ragging session to initiate them. These sessions are often friendly and enjoyable but at times they become rather ugly and worrisome when some of the senior students go overboard. Poor freshies have ended with misadventures and mishaps. Luckily for me none of these ever happened and in fact, I became very close to some of these seniors who ragged me during both my Pre-university and Pre-medical days. Two of the most prominent raggers, I still remember were Dr. Abel Arumugam who later became a general surgeon and his future wife, Dr. Gomathi, a beautiful lady who became an ophthalmic surgeon. I had two strange experiences with Dr. Gomathi in my life. Firstly, she became my senior when I entered Stanley medical college in Chennai and secondly I attended her funeral when she passed away in 2014 in Kuala Lumpur. What a strange coincidence I met this person at the beginning of my college days and at the end of her life!! Life on board during the next four days was full of fun and entertainment. I managed to make friends with several passengers especially the new students who were on board like me.

Trouble With Customs

We reached Nagapattinam the first port of call in Madras located in the South East of that state on the 7th day of sailing. The next morning, we berthed at Madras city, our final destination. The first thing I noticed and felt was the hot weather and the intolerable heat that I have never experienced

before. This was the beginning of summer and I was caught right smack under the heat wave. I tried to get out of the Port early since there was a large crowd. Unfortunately, it was not to be and I faced my first harassment on trying to clear customs.

It was a known fact the Indian customs officials were real tough often harassing passengers especially their own Indian nationals who were coming back from overseas. India was poor then and there were several restrictions on the types of goods allowed in and the hefty fines imposed on electronic goods brought in. The customs, in particular the enforcement officials, were feared by all because of their tough attitude and the 100 per cent checks they under take on the incoming and outgoing passengers from their country.

I was one of the unlucky ones that day!! I was suddenly asked to move from the routine line of custom examination by one of the enforcement officers who led me to a special room.

Much to my shock and dismay, two officers, drilled me with several tough and impertinent questions!! I just did not know why they were being tough with me probing me with several unnecessary questions especially after seeing two tins wrapped and marked 'Lena' and 'MGR' in my bag.

The reasons I discovered only after a 100% physical check up and when my local guardian Dr. Anandaraman arrived. He was the Head of the largest Eye Hospital of Madras and with some authority he came with a Senior custom officer to rescue me from the harassment in the hands of those two enforcement officers. I was feeling embarrassed and really lost in a strange country and absolutely grateful to my guardian.

Letchumanan Chettiar

The name Lena I learnt later, was the short form for Letchumanan Chettiar, a famous film producer at that point of time and MGR was meant to be the famous M.G. Ramachandran, one of the most renowned South Indian actor who eventually left acting and became the Chief Minister of Madras in 1977. Madras was later renamed Tamilnadu. Sadly, he passed away in 1987.

MGR apart from being an actor was also a member of Dravida Munnetra Kazhagam, then the ruling party in Madras, having won the state elections in 1967 after twenty years of Congress party rule since India's Independence.

Nevertheless, the Federal government was still under Congress rule and the customs department like anywhere else was under the Federal government!! Likewise, Lena, apart from being a film producer was also in the list of the customs department. The two tins that I carried for them was from one Shanmugam Chettiar from Singapore a close friend of theirs. The two tins I carried apparently contained special medication for them.

My guardian related the story to me when I was released from their dreadful customs interrogation. I was very cross with my father for putting me through such trauma. Once outside the customs, I was greeted by two burly and tall student leaders who introduced themselves as Sadasivam and Manjit Singh and that they were from All India Malaysian Students Association (AIMSA) and were there to greet us and offer any assistance if needed. As I already had my guardian there to receive me, I thanked them for their offer and left not realising that I would be meeting them very often especially Sadasivam who I later realised was fondly nicknamed 'Bapa Malaysia' by Malaysian students studying in Madras for his friendly and helpful nature.

Dr. K. Sadasivam - Popularly known as 'Bapa Malaysia' by the Malaysian students in chennai

Late Manjit Singh

My 1968, Malaysian PUC Classmates in Loyola college Chennai.

My Guardians And Network Of Friends

I next met Dr. Ramakrishnan, who was also there at the port to receive me. He was the youngest brother of Dr. Anandaraman whom I had met in 1961, when he accompanied the famous singer Seerkazhi S. Govindarajan to Malaysia on his concerts that had been organised by my father throughout West Malaysia and Singapore. Dr. Ramakrishnan had become a close friend of my father and that was the reason he and his brother were appointed as my local guardians.

Subsequently in the years to come, Dr. Ramakrishnan became a great friend of mine more than a guardian and we enjoyed several good moments during the next 50 years till his death in 2010. We arrived at Dr. Anandaraman's house where I was supposed to be staying for the next three months till I found a place for my Pre university in a college and accommodation in the college hostel. I was introduced to Mrs. Anandaraman. a bubbly lady with whom I would be sharing many laughable and tense moments in the next forty-five years together with their two daughters Vidya and Priya. Both of them became doctors in the later years with Dr.Vidya having passed away twenty years ago.

One of the first gentlemen I met in Dr. Anandaraman's house was Mr. Meenakshi Sundaram Chettiar, a close friend of both Dr. Ramakrishnan and my father. He often stayed there as a guest whenever he was in Madras city. As he was my roommate in their house he became a good friend and an elderly adviser during my stay in India.

Having settled in the oppressive humidity of Madras city that was at times intolerable, the next

Late Mr& Mrs Govindan Nair who were known to me during my student days in Chennai

Late Mr.& Mrs Govindan Nair with their children L to R.Ramachandran, his wife Premah, daughter Lakshmi and her husband Sushilan

Dr.Ramakrishnan in the 70s

obvious step was to look for one of the best colleges in the city for my Pre university course. There were several famous colleges in the city like Loyola, Christian and New College that were popular among Malaysian students. I filed my applications to all the colleges but obviously I was hoping for the better ones to get my admission. As the colleges would only open in June, I had ample time to discover the city which was historical and huge and to meet all of my father's known friends including Lena.I delivered the two tins for which he was immensely grateful not realising for a moment the ordeal I had to go through at the customs for his sake.

My guardian during my student days in Chennai. Dr.V.Anandaraman,an Opthamologist and his wife Anusuya Anandaraman.

At the wedding reception of Dr.Vidya the eldest daughter of Dr.Anandaraman to Dr.Gowrishanker.With the family of Late Seerkazhi Govindaeajan the famous playback singer of Tamil films.

Kumar S/o Tan Sri N.S. Maniam

Dr. A.Chandramogan

Our Kula Koil Theevanur Vinayagar Temple. With youngest Sitthappa Arumugam Chettiar and relative Thirumalai

My Village

Our Kula Deivam Mayilam Murugan Temple.

Athivakkan Kothandaramar Temple. Main donor Rengasamy Chettiar / Nadesan Chettiar and family

I was also able to make my first trip to our native village of Kalathur, the native place of my late grandfather Rengasamy Chettiar and Keelathivakkam village where he had finally settled and acquired more than 150 acres of agricultural lands. Both the villages faced each other and they were exactly 100 km South of Madras city towards. Trichy, another big town about 250kms from Madras.

Dr. Ramakrishnan drove me to my village in his Austin A70, a huge out-dated car. Those days the number of cars were few and the models were very limited. The most famous was Ambassador, followed by Fiat and Standard Herald, all of which were out-dated models and manufactured locally.

Before we left Madras city we bought fruits, flowers and sweets all to be given away to my relatives in my native village. On arrival at Keelathivakkam, I stopped in front of my grandfather's tomb to say my prayers. Within minutes the curious villagers crowded around me and wanted to know who I was.

Kalatthur House

Keezh Athivaakkam House

In Keezh Athivaakkam Kodhandaramar Temple with my grand mother Madam Kuppammal and relatives. Large portion of the temple construction was done with donations from my family members and I

When they were informed they became excited and started enquiring about my father, who I believe was well liked by them all for his generosity.

I was brought to my grandfather's house or rather a bungalow which seemed too huge for a village. On reaching the house, I was greeted by my step grandmother Kuppammal (the second wife of my grandfather) and a host of uncles, aunties and cousins all smiling broadly. After the usual formality of introduction and handing over of gifts, we sat down for a tasty village meal, my first village meal consisting of country chicken, goat meat and eggs.

My grandmother was such a loving person and I became fond of her and attached to her in the

y wife Renu with my mother's sisters Madam
angam, Madam Kamalam with her husband
ttu Chettiar at our land in Thozupedu

With my mother's sisters Madam Thangam, Madam Kamalam
with her husband Pattu Chettiar at our land in Thozupedu

years to come not forgetting the many visits to the village to receive additional funds from her for my expenses!! She was the matriarch of the family in India in the absence of my grandfather who was travelling between India and Malaysia till he passed away in 1964. She took care of agriculture together with my uncles, her sons Rajamanickam, Dorai and Arumugam. Her eldest son Subramaniam was in Malaysia helping in our provision business.

We left for madras city later in the evening after a long get to know session with my relatives.

Back in the city, I decided to have a look at our own bungalow which my father had bought in the name of my mother It was at 6 P Warren Road a renowned street where several prominent actors and known political leaders had their residences. Unfortunately, our bungalow had fallen under the draconian rent control act brought about by the tenants who were staying there and paying very poor rentals which was being collected by Meenakshisundaram who was the power of Attorney for my mother. Several attempts to evacuate them failed. We even tried political influence but in vain. The bungalow was old and run down but obviously it could fetch better rentals if we could decontrol the premises and found new tenants. I was told it would take another two years before we could get all the tenants out of there. After exerting much political and police pressure we managed to release the bungalow from

My youngest Sitthi Late Mallika with her family

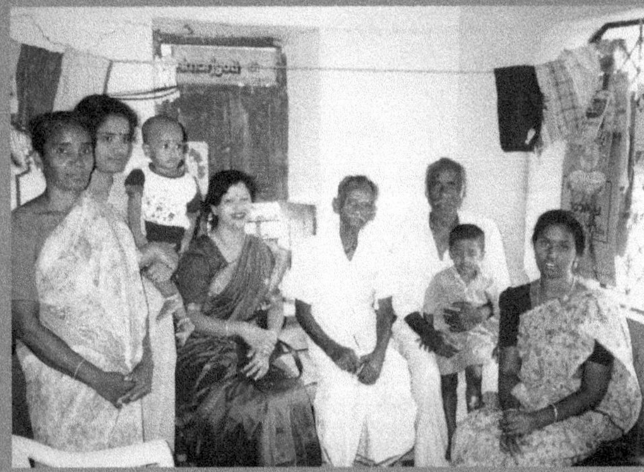

My wife with Mr. Ramasamy who was our long term employee and his family members

the rent control act only to sell the bungalow in 1973 to fulfil part of my father's desire to become a film producer!!!

Dr. Ramakrishnan and Meenakshisundaram who were shareholders in a pharmaceutical company called Venus labs where my father too had a share decided to go on a marketing trip throughout Madras renamed Tamil Nadu by the ruling DMK government

We left on a fine morning and travelled across Tamil Nadu covering quite a distance meeting several general practitioners on the way promoting the Venus laboratory's products quite apart from stopping at the various temples on the way for prayers. The temples were awesome, historical and I marvelled at the structures and the construction some of which were more than a thousand years. We started off with the famous Kanjipuram temple and traversed across the equally famous temples of Seerkazhi, Chidambaram, Trichy, Thanjavur, Kumbakonam, Madurai, Pillaiyarpatti and Rameswaram. Our trip which took us more than ten days was very enjoyable because of the jovial nature of both Dr. Ramakrishnan and Meenakshisundaram. The temples were an awesome discovery for me we stopped at Meenakshisundaram's native place called Kilasevalpatti in Chettinad named in honour of the famous Chettiar community who were known for their business prowess, acumen and intelligence for many centuries.

Sitthappa Subramaniam Chettiar with his wife and his family

The Nagarathaars or more commonly called 'Nattukottai Chettiars' were well known for their business ventures across the seven seas and had established themselves as credible traders for several centuries in most south east Asian countries like Burma, Ceylon (Srilanka), Malaya, Singapore and Vietnam. For their business acumen they had been recognised by the British Empire who had ruled India for more than three centuries and even accorded them a statehood known as 'Chettinad' (Land of Chettiars). The best known of them was called 'Sir Raja Annamalai' who was the first to be bestowed the title of 'Rajah of Chettinad in 1929' by the British Empire. They were not only good business people but they were equally great philanthropists having established several charitable and educational institutions in India particularly in Tamil Nadu. I had the distinctive honour of knowing the 3rd Rajah of Chettinad Mr. M.A.M. Ramasamy Chettiar who was one of

My Sitthappa Late Rajamanikam Chettiar, Wife Late Thanapakiyam. His son Siva with his wife

My Sitthappa Late Durai Chettiar with his family

With my youngest Sitthappa Arumugam Chettiar and his wife

the Patrons of the 'Overseas Students Association of Madras' (OSA) when I was the President from 1973 to 1974.

Chettiar is basically a clan in India one among many thousands in India even today. Surprisingly there were many sub clans from each clan. My family also belongs to the Chettiar community not the Nagarathaars but from the 'Ayiravaisiar' group that is a much larger group than the Nagarathaars. It would be foolhardy for me to explain about the clan and caste system that existed since time immemorable among the Hindus in India. It would be too long a story and would never make sense to the modern world. Nevertheless, it was rather unfortunate but interesting enough when I was first inducted into the discovery of the caste system in my life in India. My father had never shown any interest in the caste system neither has he ever spoken about it to us. He had never shown any difference to his fellow human beings especially among his Indian friends and followers.

In Madras city, now known as Chennai, I used to follow Dr. Ramakrishnan to his private clinic in the evenings in Chindadaripet. I met several interesting personalities there including famous actors like T.S. Baliah and M.R. Radha who were doyens of the Tamil film industry. They were his patients and I had the opportunity to spend several hours with them discussing with them the film industry, their roles and about the various actors and actresses some of them were very revealing, interesting and sometimes shocking!! I had always been interested and crazy about the movie industry since young and many a time have I dreamt about becoming an actor myself!!

I had the privilege to meet several other personalities through Dr. Ramakrishnan. People like Dr. Rathinavel Subramaniam, a very famous and respected Physician at that time, the Director of Medical education and a few politicians including the famous Mr C.N. Annadurai, fondly known as 'Arigner Anna' and then Chief Minister of Tamil Nadu during a dinner given in honour of a Malaysian student delegation's visit to Madras at Dr. Anandaraman's house. The chief de mission was none other than S. Subramaniam who later became the Secretary General of Malaysian Indian Congress (MIC), and a Deputy Minister and my personal friend. My father and Mr. R. Balakrishnan (RTM Head of Indian Section) arranged the dinner while Dr. Ramakrishnan and Dr. Anandaraman, personal physicians and friends to Mr Annadurai were to host it and invite Mr. Annadurai as the chief guest. That was the first and last time I met Mr. Annadurai. He later fell ill with throat cancer and while being treated in the USA he succumbed to the disease in February 1969. I have never seen such a mammoth funeral procession till then!! (It became a Guinness record for the largest funeral gathering!!). He was a popular writer, an eloquent orator, an honest leader and above all a good human being revered by the Tamils not only in Tamil Nadu but also throughout the world.

My Sitthappa Late Arumugam Chettiar with his wife and Family

At my grand father's tomb in Keelathivakkam

My 1st year in Madras Medical College 1969 Batch of classmates.Sitting in front row 2nd from right

In Medical College

It was early June 1968, and the first college to accept my application was the famous Christian college in Tambaram about 30 km away from Chennai. The college was at that time famous for its 'extracurricular activities' than academic achievement. It was where the children of the 'Rich and the famous' wanted to be!! Since this was the first college that offered admission, I went and paid my admission and hostel fees immediately and waited for the opening day, which was never to be!! Two weeks later, I received my second offer letter from the famous Loyola college in Nungambakkam which was within city limits and about 5 km away from Dr. Anandaraman's residence, in Kilpauk, a famous residential area. The decision was simple and quick. Dr. Anandaraman decided it was Loyola College, I paid my admission and hostel fees again and waited for the opening.

Though I never got a chance to study in Christian college during my subsequent years I became close to many of the Christian college students both Malaysians and local Indians. Many of them became famous and colourful in later years like Pratap Pothen, the famous actor and director of both Tamil and Malayalam films.

Loyola College, Chennai, P.U.C. 1968-1969

1st Year Medicine in Madras Medical College - 1969-1970

I became close to two students from Christian College a year later. One a Malaysian student called Gunaseelan whom I ragged and another a local student called Kumar Calappa whose family became very friendly during my stay in India. Having got myself admitted in Loyola College and the hostel, the first person I came into contact was Arichandra, a Malaysian student who was my neighbour in the hostel. He became a doctor and a General in the Malaysian Army later. I discovered there were around 20 Malaysian students studying in the college in the various courses but mostly doing Pre University. Some of the senior students especially Malaysians acquainted themselves with us through mild ragging sessions. Loyola a Jesuit college with its Christian background was known equally for its academic results and strict discipline. Anyone crossing the limits was punished adequately by both suspension and expulsion.

As I was already a pure science student and had sat for two of the pure science subjects, chemistry and biology in the senior Cambridge exams, I found the going in Pre U relatively easy. During my Pre U in Loyola despite discipline being there, I managed to sneak out to gallivant at night with Ramanathan, a medical student and Rajkumar who was waiting to get into medical college with Arichandra's help. Besides the guards were easily won over with monetary tips!

Despite all this enjoyment, I stayed focussed in my studies and managed to score well in my Pre

From 2nd year medicine to final year in Stanley Medical College

U exams held in April 1969.I scored distinctions for my biology and chemistry and a very decent A plus (just below distinction) for Physics, the subject I detested most. I even managed to score an A plus for my second language French, though only a pass was needed.

The results were out in early June 1969 and we had to apply immediately for our medical seats that were in such a big demand then. Not only did you need good results, but needed to have good political connections and loads of money for these politicians. Thank god with my good results and the strong political influence my father had with the local DMK politicians especially, Mr.Murasoli Maran, my medical seat was assured. Mr Murasoli Maran was my father's close friend and nephew of the then Chief Minister of Tamil Nadu 'Kalaignar M.Karunanidhi.' My father had always maintained his relationship with several politicians who were from both Congress and DMK for several years. 1n

My good friends during my college days in Chenna in the early 70s. (L to R) Datuk Dr.Athi, late Dr.Amirthasingam and Gen. Datuk Dr. Mohandas

1960, when my father got his two sisters Rukumani and Parvathy married in our Keelathivakkam village he even managed to bring electricity for the first time to our village through the help of a congress minister in Madras called Mr. Ramiah Pillai. He was the brother of Mr.Sinniah Pillai, a very prominent businessman and a close family friend of ours from Johor Bahru, my hometown.

Those days there were many ways to apply for medical seats and Malaysian students were particularly smart in knowing the different ways.

There were seats offered on a government to government basis at the federal level called nomination or cultural scholarship seats. They were limited in numbers and were generally awarded to Malaysian students with excellent PUC results. Here too you needed some amount of influence with the federal government at Delhi. The Tamil Nadu government used to offer about 5 medical seats to Malaysian students of Tamil origin. Here again it was based on our results and political influence that we had, quite apart from the money that we offered. There were also other ways and methods of getting seats by Malaysians who did not get the required results to apply for medical seats in government colleges and they were familiar with all of these.My father used some of these methods and helped many of his friends' children from Malaysia to get them medical seats.There were many issues in doing this and my father had to coordinate all these in securing medical seats for

The All India Malaysian Students' Association (Madras Branch) 1970. Dr.Athimulam as Chairman with his members including Guna, Arasu, Ameen, Victor, Sena and Manokary all of my many friends in Chennai and later in Malaysia

several of his friends' children from different parts of Malaysia but mainly from Johor state.

Not wanting to take any chance, I applied under both the categories. With my good results and thanks to my father's influence at both federal and state level my application under both the categories were successful. Apart from political influence, one had to know the members of the interview committee most of them being from the medical fraternity. This was taken care of by Dr. Anandaraman and Dr. Ramakrishnan who were both influential in their own ways.

At the end, I was admitted to first MBBS in Madras Medical College, thanks to the help given by Mr.Murasoli Maran and Kalaignar Karunanidhi, the Chief Minister of Tamilnadu both of whom I would always remember with gratitude in my life. My father had landed in Madras immediately after I had made my application for medical college and stayed on for a month till the results were announced to ensure my medical seat. It cost my father heavily. He had booked 2 cottages in Asoka hotel one of the better hotels in Chennai at that time to entertain various political and personal friends spending an exorbitant Rupees 35,000 on

Dr.K.M.Ganesan,my close friend and classmate from 1969 to 1975 in medical with his family.He is a paediatrician at Gudiyatham. Tamil Nadu..

The late Shanmugam and his wife Saras. He was the brother in law of J.Sarangapany of Singapore and travelled with me on board M.V.Chidambaram during my return journey to Malaysia from Chennai during my college holidays in 1971.

the hotel bills This was despite the fact that Murasoli Maran had already assured him a seat for me in the initial stage of his arrival in Madras city. It was unnecessary for my father to have stayed on for that long but that was my father for you, never wanting to take any chance with his son's education and future!!!

While there were more than 8 government medical colleges then in Tamilnadu, I was placed in Stanley Medical college a 150 years old prestigious college right in the heart of the city at the request of my guardian, Dr.Anandaraman, who was then the head of Ophthalmology department in Stanley. However, my 1st year posting was in Madras Medical Collage in the city where my life took the first important turn!!

For the first time in my life, I failed in my 1st year exams and that too in my favourite Chemistry paper. I was retained, and had to sit for my September paper and got through.

In my first year, I became close to local Indian students namely Ganesan, Doraisamy, Nisar and a few others. It was a coincidence but all three of them also failed in their first year exams despite not having any problems like I had!! They too got through in September along with me.

I became friends with a few Malaysian students like Ehambaram and seniors like Athimulam who became a pathologist in the Malaysian army and Mohandas who became a consultant and a General in the Malaysian army.

Coming into Stanley was totally a different experience. Whilst the students of Madras Medical were from the upper strata of society and from the city, the students in Stanley were mostly from the districts and from agricultural families. Stanley was located in Washermenpet near Royapuram one of the poorest area of

Madras city. The saddest part of Stanley was, it was caste ridden and was controlled by the effluent Gounders and the schedule caste. This often led to caste tension resulting in serious fights between the 2 groups leading to closure of the college for a few days in a year. The smaller caste groups often were caught between the cross fires of these 2 groups. It was rather shameful especially as it was happening in a medical college.

After my PUC exams, I used to spend considerable time with a group of Malaysians students in a lodge quite close to my guardian Dr. Ramakirushnan's clinic in Chindadripet. It was a dingy, run down lodge but good enough for their budget. The guys were Rajkumar, Sukumaran in his BSc.class, Balu in Veterinary, Kumar Maniam in B. Com and a few others.

This is when I met Guna, who joined Christian college and did his B.Com degree there. Chandramogan who became a dentist and Hariprasad who also did B.Com. They were all Malaysians and our juniors and were ragged by us only to become good friends later. All of us used to stay in this single crammed up room sharing our meals and watching old Malayalam movies in the evenings in a rundown theatre called New Elphinstone or Casino theatre to watch the latest English movies. Next to Elphinstone theatre was a famous ice cream parlour Jaffar Cafe where we enjoyed so many different types of ice creams at such low prices. We used to patronize Muniyandy

Mr.&.Mrs.Jeyapal Naidu with Dr.Athimulam's and my classmate Dr.Gnambal's wedding reception.We were entertained to many days of sumptuous food at Uncle & aunty Jeyapal naidu's home on many occasions during our college days in Chennai. It was during on one of these Deepavali dinners in their home in Chennai that i met my wife Renu.

and Ponnusamy vilas- two famous South Indian restaurants with our 'tiffin carrier' to buy enough food with the little money and shared among ourselves. What comradeship and what a way we lived!! It was real fun, though all of us did not have much to spend and used to share whatever we had. Most of the Malaysian students who came to India those days were those who wanted to be doctors more so because of their parent's wishes but many who didn't make it, opted out for other courses like Veterinary science, Dental, B.Sc, B.com and even automobile engineering!! It was estimated that there were some 50,000 Malaysian students

Late Mr& Mrs J.Sarangapany, a close family friend in Singapore

Late Mr.Sarangapany of Singapore with (L to R) Guna, Tan sri Haranarayan, Lawyer Ganesan, Viji, Kalai and Jega.

studying in different parts of India those days, many in way-out places! Malaysian students were adventurous in nature and they went in search of medical college seats throughout India.

As I used to go to my guardian's clinic in the evenings to be with him, I became close and familiar with many of his patients. One of them was a customs officer Govindan Nair and his family who stayed in the same locality. His children Ramachandran, later migrated to Singapore, his daughter Lakshmi married Susheelan a Malaysian and settled in Malaysia. Gopi was working in merchant ships and disappeared one day without any trace during one of his journeys. Both Ramachandran and Lakshmi have remained as our family friends till date.

Mrs.Govindan was quite fond of me and used to invite me quite often for meals in their home.

Dr. Ramakrishnan was guardian for quite a few Malaysian students, like Vijayaratnam from Johor Bahru and in Madras Medical College and Mahendran who was in the Madras Veterinary College. They came to the clinic during weekends basically to meet and have special food cooked regularly by a cook from a famous Gajendra Vilas restaurant in Mount Road. Dr.Palaniappan a close friend of Dr. Ramakrishnan , was practicing a few doors away from his clinic. He used to join us for some of our drinking and eating sessions.

Stanley medical college was not only of the oldest (150 years) and renowned medical institution in India, it was also a college that had produced several prominent physicians and surgeons of Indian and international repute. Some of the famous personalities were Prof S Kalyanasundaram (neurosurgeon), Prof K.V. Thiruvengadam (Physician), Prof Vengatasamy (Plastic Surgeon), Prof Madanagopal (Physician), Dr. Solomon Victor (physician) and many more

including my own classmate Dr. Surendran who created one of the best liver transplant centres in India in Stanley when he became the head of the Hepatic Biliary unit in his later years.

My time in Stanley started off with the usual ragging sessions by seniors.

Many local students like Ganesan, Nisar and Veera Narayanan all were friendly except for Malick Harun and Jerome Pereira who later became accommodating.

I had Malaysian friends too like Valliappen and Bala both of whom are from Klang, Malaysia. There was my junior, a Malaysian student by the name of Rajapathi who became a doctor, a Penang MIC leader and later became a state minister. This was really surprising to me because as a student he used to avoid all social functions especially among Malaysians and shied away from us. More so when I was in MIC and when I was elected to the Central Working Committee twice in 1984 and 1987, he as a MIC branch Chairman then used to advise me to keep away from politics!! What a turn of event when he became active in politics and became a state Minister.Another junior was Subramaniam also from Klang who became a general practitioner in his home -town.

Yet another colleague of mine from Stanley, Dr. Jayabalan joined the opposition in Malaysia and became elected to the Penang state assembly in 2013.

My junior, Hariprasad was a Senior Banker

Having failed in my chemistry paper in my first year due to my 'extracurricular' distractions I was determined to do well during my following years in college. I did Anatomy, physiology and biochemistry papers in my 2nd year of medicine, considered as one of the longest and toughest years among the 5 ½ years of medical course. I cleared all my 3 papers in my first attempt and in fact I was one of the top students in my biochemistry exam which I wrote during the first 6 months of my 2nd year. Having got through my biochemistry exam I decided to return to Malaysia after 2 years during my summer holidays and to be away from the blistering summer heat. I had not gone back home since coming to India. I spent my holidays travelling within India especially to Bangalore, a cosmopolitan city where the climate was much cooler, and much preferred by Malaysians. I had a Malaysian student friend in Bangalore called Vijayan Naidu with whom I used to stay in Bangalore although I had a paternal aunty called Rukumani married to a lawyer Narayanamoorthy.

During my return trip to Malaysia which was on board the MV Chidambaram a modern ship that was plying between Tamilnadu and Malaysia then and was named after one of the famous freedom fighters Chidambaram Pillai from Tamil Nadu who fought the British for India's independence. He was also known as the first person to ply a ship against the British East India Company during the fight for India's independence movement. What a great and strong figure he must have been! His life history became a Tamil movie later and he was portrayed by the most famousTamil actor, Sivaji Ganesan.

The journey as usual, was enjoyable with so many Malaysian students returning home for their holidays. Many of us including those from far south also landed in Penang in order to travel back home quickly by various modes of transport. If we had waited to land in Port Klang or Singapore to travel back to home, it would have taken us either one or two more full days before we reached home. I had during my journey on the ship met a gentleman by the name of Shanmugam from Singapore who happened to be the brother in law of Mr. Sarangapany, my father's good friend in Singapore (not to confuse with Tamil Vel Sarangapany who owned the Singapore daily Tamil Murasu). I became close not only to Shanmugam but Sarangapany's entire family in Singapore over the years. His children named Vijaya who later married Maran, Jega who became a dentist, Guna who became an accountant and married Rajesh and the youngest Kalai who married Raj a businessman. They became more like a family to me and our friendship continues till today. Surprisingly, I discovered that Mr. Sarangapany was the paternal uncle of my friend Guna from Christian college!!

Trouble Brews At Home

Reaching home by taxi the next morning was a joy especially seeing my mother.

The next two months I spent with my family having delicious home cooked food and meeting classmates especially with Donald Choo. He became the Director of Sales of EON one of the leading Proton car (Malaysian car) distribution companies in Malaysia in his later years. He still keeps in touch with me. Many of my other classmates had moved on to different universities to pursue their education. My Indian student group from school days had moved on to take up various government and private jobs.

I realised the financial situation of my family and its depth of seriousness. Both our retail provision businesses at 32, Jalan Segget and our grinding mill business and at 3, Jalan Ah Fook had been wound down the previous year due to business difficulties and the premises rented out. The only retail business that was still being run was originally founded by Manickam Chettiar, one of those who had worked as a manager under my late grandfather and moved on to manage his own provision

M.V. Chidambaram

business successfully in the fifties in Kluang. After he passed away in the early sixties, with no one to manage his business my father had to take over at his family's request. Manickam chettiar's wife and only daughter Radha were regular guests in our households for all our family functions as much as we were their guests in their home in Kluang. This friendship has remained till today with Radha, her husband Raju the son of Thirumeny Pather, a goldsmith who was one of my father's earliest friends when he came back from India in 1947 and their 3 children.

Imagine a multimillion- dollar business empire crumbling to nothing after 50 years!! Here was my father who despite being uneducated turned his father's small business into multi- diversified conglomerate at the age of 37 only to lose it all when he was only 45. Call it mismanagement or fate, but I attributed it to his poor management and neglect especially after his involvement in public and political activities. Now I believe my father was managing his finances and looking after our families which included my uncle Kandasamy's family consisting of his wife Chandra and his 5 children - Mohan, Rengasamy (Babu) Muthukumar, Viji and Uma. Father was managing from the collection from the tenancy of our 2 shops, our provision shop at Kluang and a small taxi company that he had with 2 other partners. It must have been a very trying time indeed!

While in Stanley Medical College - 1972

Back to college and distractions

My sister Sarojini had just completed her senior Cambridge exams and was ready to leave with me to India to further her studies. As my sister was travelling with me, we were booked to fly on our first maiden flight in our lives despite our family's financial problems. We flew from Singapore to Chennai by Air India that was quite popular then. She got admitted for her PUC into SIET Women's college, popular among Malaysian students and in time completed her B.Com degree.

At the beginning of my second year in medical college, I went to stay in a newly constructed beautiful student hostel called World University Centre in Harrington Road specifically meant for foreign students. Here I became active as the Chairman of the Cinema club and had the pleasure of inviting several cinema personalities like director K. Balachandar, actor Gemini Ganesh and actress Sowcar Janaki as our guests when we screened movies in our auditorium. I enjoyed this role very much as I was a crazy movie fan since young.

Overseas students' association picnic - 1972 (Shanmugam, Velayutham, Manickam, Chandran, Sashi, Ramasamy, Soma)

During my stay there, many of my Malaysian friends who were studying out of Madras city used to come to stay with me during their holidays, as my comfortable hostel was centrally located in the city. There were three other Malaysian students Henry, Dev Kumar and Ravi who used to stay there. Henry was trying for many years to get into a medical college but did not make it. Ravi became a doctor and a surgeon along with Devkumar who too became a surgeon. Both Henry and Devkumar were great singers and we used to spend quite a bit of time singing away our blues in the evenings quite often joined by my outstation friends. There were many other foreign students from different countries staying there and I was quite friendly with most of them. I remember one cute little girl around 13 years old coming around to our hostel often from the neighbourhood to chat with us. She was Manjula who later became a very famous and beautiful actress of the South Indian film world and subsequently married actor Vijayakumar who was a hero and later a character actor in the Tamil films. Manjula has since passed away.

While both my studies and my other interests in life was going smoothly, I became involved in the various activities of AIMSA and OSA of which I became the President in 1973. The third medical year was considered to be an easy going year since there was only a single Exam subject, Pharmacology. As usual I became a very active President. Since school days I have been active organising various social, cultural and charitable activities, the best of which was to raise a substantial amount of Rupees 25,000 (which was huge for those days!!) for the Chief Minister's relief fund as the President of Overseas Students Association.

We were lucky to have two famous Industrialists as our Patrons Mr.H.C. Kothari of the Kothari group and Mr.M.A.M. Ramasamy of the Chettinad

family and was also the Sheriff of Madras then. This gave our OSA members and my committee an opportunity to be invited to Chettinad palace of M.A.M. Ramasamy in Chennai for their functions and various festivals. Their patronage opened up several doors for us and helped us in raising the 25,000 rupees from the cultural show organised in aid of the Chief Minister's fund. Another gentleman by the name of Mr.Nannu, one of the top management executive of Indian Oil Corporation became good friends and was very helpful to us.

The show was held at SIET college auditorium a famous ladies' college in Chennai where most of the Malaysian girls including my sister Sarojini and my future wife to be Ranuga Devy were also students!! The show was a big hit and I was one of the performers singing for the first time on stage the famous 'baila' song which originated from Srilanka and was very popular then in South

My Shenguntha clan - Cook Mathew, N. Venu, Nimmi, PK Venu, Logan, Soma

India especially in Tamilnadu. Various versions and verses in the various languages had been coined and were particularly popular among the student community.

ICCR (Indian council for cultural Relationship) a federal government agency worked closely with OSA to promote activities among foreign students. One of activities was a study tour sponsored entirely by them during our December holidays. I led a team of 30 students mostly Malaysians consisting of both males and females. The trip turned out to be a very enjoyable one from Bangalore, Mysore, Pune, and Bombay where we celebrated our new year. It was a lot of fun especially as many of us were also friends. I was particularly close to Guna, Mary, Absolom, Shirley, John, Sena, and Kurien who were all my committee members. Three of the non -committee members were Rajkumar, Vasantha and Kumar Calappa a close friend of

Big Temple, Tanjore

Guna and the only Indian Student who was invited to come along with us.

Apart from being a regular guest in Dr. Anandaraman's house throughout my entire stay in India for regular meals and their functions, I was also a familiar face not only in Kumar Calappa's house but also in the home of a couple by the name of Mr. and Mrs. Jayapal Naidu, Both were known to my father. Their house in Nungambakkam was the meeting place for many of the Malaysian and Singaporean students residing there namely Babu (Sabai) aunty Jayapal's brother, Malliga who became a dentist and married Babu and later settled in Adelaide, Australia. Vijayakumar became a doctor and settled in Canada. Manokary became a veterinarian and settled in Malaysia and Athimulam in particular who used to reside there with them. Aunty Jayapal was an excellent cook and we used to have a great time with good meals and wonderful parties. It was a happening place with Mohandas and Amirthasingam who were both Malaysian medical students, joining us. Dr. Amirthasingam has since passed away.

I did not stay in a hostel after my PUC days but in lodges and apartments with Malaysian students except during exams when I used to move back to

Stanely hostel to study for my exams. I had stayed in Sudarshan lodge during my 1st year, in WUS during my 2nd year, in an apartment in Santhome in my 3rd year and in two different apartments in Shenoy Nagar during my 4th and houseman years.

I was residing in an apartment in Santhome in 1973 during my third year of medicine with a few Malaysian students called Ravi, Rajendran, (both of whom were doing automobile engineering) Pathmanaban did commercial studies, Letchumanan became a lawyer, both of whom have since passed away. Venugopal became a Pharmaceutical representative and Saga, a doctor and a successful General practition has also passed away. Opposite to our apartment were two other Malaysians, Nathan, who became a doctor and Sam Barr, who became a senior company Executive and has since passed away. These were fun loving guys and we used to have several roof top parties with singing, dancing and drinking. Quite close to our apartment was sea view lodge in Santhome famous for its Malaysian students like Krishnamoorthy who became a doctor, Jeeva, a Pharmacist and several others who often joined us in our parties. We have all remained as friends till now! Thamby a Malaysian medical student was also a regular guest. He is a GP and resides in Ipoh presently.

During my stay in an apartment in Shenoy nagar during my final year of medical course, my housemates were mostly juniors including Venugopal my brother. The guys were PK Venu, Sashi, Guna all of whom became plantation managers and Soma who became a doctor. We used to have some outstation friends like Vijayan Naidu from Bangalore with whom I used to stay in Bangalore during my holidays. The guys used to give me lot of respect but nevertheless we used to have fun together. There were several guests at our apartment where they used to enjoy the food cooked by our cook called George who was more of a friend of ours.

I was close to Kumar Calappa and his family. Guna and I were both quite regularly invited to their home for meals apart from the luxurious Black label whisky (which was a rarity then) which uncle Calappa used to serve. They were Coorgis and originated from the cool hills of Coorg in the state of Mysore. The Coorgis were known to be a brave clan, warm and hospitable. We were often invited to travel with them to Coorg for many of their family functions and weddings that were really grand and very entertaining. We were treated by all of them as part of their family and became close to many of them especially Vijay, Madhu, Kasturi, Asha, Nina and Tulsi all of whom were cousins of Kumar. Kumar himself was in love with a Coorgi by the name of Bollu, a petite gentle girl whom he married subsequently. Both Guna and I have been close to Bollu even after both uncle and aunty Calappa and Kumar passed away many years later.

In 1972, my brother Venugopal came to pursue his studies. He was admitted to Pachaiyappa's college

where he took up B. Com just like my sister Sarojini in SIET.

I was particularly fond of Rajkumar whom I had met in 1968 and who had subsequently joined Tanjore Medical College in 1970. We became close friends. We used to stay together in a lodge nick named DMK whenever he came to Madras city during his holidays. I used to travel quite often to Tanjavur about 250 km away from Madras city to spend some of my holidays with him. He was staying outside in rented houses with a couple of Malaysian students studying there. One among them was Mohd Hanifa a Malaysian Indian student who was my friend for more than 30 years only to end up breaking our long lasting friendship over a business deal.

My trips to Tanjore were basically to spend good time with Rajkumar and Haniffa, apart from visiting the Temples in Tanjore and its neighbouring towns which they were famous for. One of the most famous was the 'Big Temple' built by the famous Chola emperor Raja Raja Cholan in the 11th century. Its history and the construction is an architectural marvel even today!

The Chola Empire was one of the most famous empires of South India and both Raja Raja Cholan and in particular his son Rajendra Cholan have been credited with the conquest of the then South East Asia consisting of Malaya and Indonesia including Kalimantan in the 11th century. Their influence and conquest of Malaya has been recorded and noted in the state of Kedah by historical and archaeological findings. Unfortunately, their conquest did not last for long!! There are attempts in Malaysia to write the fascinating history but remains clouded by politics.

My father's last visit to chennai with Mr. Bala - 1973

My Father's Last Visit

In 1973 my father came for a visit to India with Mr. R. Balakrishnan from RTM. The actual reason my father had come to India was to sell his bungalow due to his financial difficulties as three of his children were in India and he needed money to finance their education. He also had plans to produce a Tamil film. That was his dream encouraged by people from the Tamil film industry, especially T.N .Balu, then a famous director of Tamil films. I tried to dissuade my father from selling the bungalow as this was the only property in my mother's name but my father was adamant about selling as he was in need of money. The price was fixed at Rupees 150,000 which was reasonable at that time but only if he had known the way the property prices would soar in Madras in the next 30 years he may have had a change of heart.

When he received the money from the sale of the bungalow he immediately got 'poojai' (prayers) for his new film in which Sowcar Janaki a famous actress then was the heroine for the main character. It was a thriller and in which one of the two main characters was a villain's role. The director was T.N.Balu whom I met during my father's stay in Madras. He knew that I was also keen in acting and one day out of the blues asked me whether I would like to act in the villain's character in my father's film which he was about to direct. I was overjoyed, as it was my dream to be an actor since I was young. He arranged for a 'screen test' a prerequisite for any wannabe actor. I came out with flying colours with a good command of Tamil as I was fluent in it.

My professors of Stanley Medical College who taught us

But the minute he mentioned this to my father as a matter of fact and praised me for passing the screen test, my father listened in silence. When T.N. Balu left he reprimanded and scolded me severely saying my duty was to become a doctor and not an actor, thus nipping my dream in the bud!! As I was dependent on my father for my living and since it was my family's dream that I become a doctor, I decided that I would complete my studies and then come back to acting but it never materialized. Deep down in my heart I have always known that I would have become a good actor if I had had the opportunity

My father's dream of becoming a film producer never took off due to the huge requirement of funding which he was not able to raise. After the prayers for the film and having two songs recorded the film was abandoned with his losses standing at Rupees twenty five thousand.

My father left Madras after banking in the balance of Rupees one hundred thousand for our studies. Though my father had always provided me enough for my living expenses during my stay in India, I was enterprising enough to make extra money for my extracurricular activities like travelling, entertaining and partying.

I had kept close contact with some of the political friends of my father after he left in 1969, the chief among them being C. Dakshnamoorthy (CDM in short) who was a personal friend of Chief Minister Karunanidhi. Using his connection, I used to secure veterinary and medical seats for one or two Malaysian students in Madras.

With my dream of becoming an actor being shattered, I continued with my studies with a determination that I would pursue my dream of

becoming an actor once I completed my studies and became a doctor for the sake of my family.

During 4th and final year there were several professors with whom I was close to. They were Dr.U. Mohamed, Professor of medicine, Dr.Jagathesan, Professor of Urology and Dr.Colin Seenivasan, Professor of Obstetrics and gynaecology. My being close to them was not planned but as it turned out they were to play important roles in my final year examinations as my internal examiners which was helpful to me to qualify as a doctor.

External examiners for the public examinations especially from the 2nd year to final year generally came from the neighbouring states of Andhra Pradesh, Karnataka (Mysore) and Kerala. Many of the examiners from Andhra used to stay with Dr. Anandaraman's house and I became close to them as I would be driving them around in Madras. I didn't have the luck to find any of them during my examinations. Nevertheless, they were helpful to some of my Malaysian friends who were failing constantly and had the good fortune to meet some of these examiners which helped them to get through their exams. This was quite normal those days to seek the help of these examiners for those students who were failing regularly in a particular examination paper.

I sat for my final year examination in April 1975 and despite being fearful, (which was normal) I got through thanks to my local professors who came in as my internal examiners in all my final clinical

Prof Dr.Mani on the right with Dr.Munaf my classmate.

examinations of medicine, surgery and obstetrics and gynaecology. With their presence my fear factor was less and that naturally helped as I was their own student and known well to them. This does not happen normally and I believe lady luck was with me!!

Having got through my exams, it was time to start my houseman-ship for one year which would qualify me to become a full fledged doctor. I began my first houseman posting in June 1975 in the obstetrics and gynaecology department under my Professor Dr. Colin Seenivasan.

Demise Of My Father

It was the early morning of 6th August 1975 when I was suddenly awakened by a hostel staff who told me that there was a long distance trunk call from Malaysia. I ran to the phone (no such thing as mobile phones during those times) and I heard my uncle Kandasamy telling me that my father had taken ill and I needed to come back. He told me that they will be sending an air ticket for me through Malaysian Airlines and for me to contact their local office. Panic and worry took over me but I found myself at the Malaysian Airlines office by 9 AM when they were just opening. There was a ticket waiting for me to pick up and leave for Kuala Lumpur but unfortunately a Japanese terrorist group by the name of Red Guards had seized control of Subang International Airport in Kuala Lumpur. This was the first time that such an event had taken place in Malaysia and this had forced the closure of the only international airport in Kuala Lumpur.

I was in a dilemma with the only option left to fly into Singapore by another airline. I did not have any cash on me and air tickets were pretty costly those days. I had to contact several of my friends to raise the required amount to buy the cheapest ticket to Singapore by Air India. I flew on 6th night to Singapore and was received by Mr. Govindasamy a personal friend of our family on 7th morning. On our one-hour journey to Johor Bahru I was constantly enquiring about my father's health condition. He was evasive and kept saying he was admitted in JB General Hospital and his condition was improving.

As we approached my home, I noticed several cars and crowds around my home. Uncle Govindasamy (as we used to call him) grabbed my hand, held it firmly and blurted out the words I least expected to hear. 'Be brave, your father has passed away'. I could not believe his words. I swung open the car door and ran into my house only to see my father's dead body. I saw my mother, hugged her and sobbed uncontrollably. It was a loss I could not bear. Suddenly my mind was clouded with so many unanswered questions. Here was my father who always wanted to see me as a doctor, lying dead without even a goodbye.

Funeral arrangements were underway, but here was a soul who had given so much of his wealth and time for others in his life but now his own family was left without any money even for his own final rites and journey. Call it misfortune or fate but that was the situation. I learnt later that the well-wishers who were there were collecting donations for his funeral but were stopped short by RTM

Mr.R. Balakrishnan who volunteered to pay for the full funeral expenses. That's true friendship for you!!

There was a huge turnout of relatives, friends, political leaders from the various communities, members from MIC and other Non Government organisations.

The Chief Minister of Johor state Dato Othman Saad, state ministers and representative of the then Prime Minister Datuk Hussein Onn who happened to be a personal friend of my father were there to pay their last respects.

It was estimated that more than 5000 people paid their last respects to him and more than 2000 people accompanied the hearse that carried his body in the funeral procession accompanied by a band organised by MIC JB branch. Apparently there has never been such a big crowd seen before for an Indian leader's funeral procession in the state of Johor. That was the kind of love and respect that my father had earned during his lifetime! MIC president Tan Sri Manickavasagam, Deputy President Datuk Athi Nagappan, Secretary General S. Subramaniam, CWC members Mr.K. Pathmanaban, Mr.V.L.Kandan, Mr.G.Vadivelu and hundreds of state and MIC National leaders led the procession. In fact, many of them accompanied the hearse in its entire 7 km journey to the Indian graveyard at Kebun Teh from my home.

We realised during our father's final rites at that Hindu cemetery, the amount of love and respect that he had commanded among his friends, well wishers, leaders of the various communities, business associates and his own peers before the final lighting of his pyre. It was most devaststing to witness so many people expressing such an emotional good bye to my father.

After my father's funeral, not only were there hundreds of my father's friends who came to pay their respects to our family but attended all the religious and prayer ceremonies.

Taking
Responsibility

As the eldest son, I realised that the entire responsibility of my family was on my shoulders. It didn't take me long to realise the financial difficulties that my late father had undergone especially during his last few years which ultimately led to his death at the young age of 48!!

Though his children were grown and were well on their way to take up the family responsibility, I believe he would not have waited for us to support him. My father's income had dropped drastically despite having had and managed several businesses during his lifetime including having been a housing developer. The irony of it was, despite having been a successful housing developer and having built more than 200 houses under the name Majidee Park (which still exists proudly in JB) there was not a single shelter left there for us when he passed away!! The only house we were staying in was also under mortgage and in poor condition.

My brothers Venugopal and Shanmugam with their wives Vasugi and Mala with my wife Renu and I.

My brother Venugopal and his wife Vasugi with their childrens Sankari, Kavitha and their grand children

Among the many successful businesses that my father had managed was a registered money lending business (which was a common business among the Chettier community) in which he had a huge customer base mainly petty traders who had borrowed money from him for their day to day business. My father had managed a very fair money lending business and he had also received deposits from many especially from the enterprising Ceylonese Tamil housewives!! They were prudent ladies who kept their savings with my father and received reasonable monthly interests from him. On going through the hundreds of IOUs (I owe you) documents, I realised there were also several land titles that had been mortgaged to my father. Visvanathan, my father's long-standing clerk said that they were never transferred despite the borrowers having defaulted nor had they repaid their loans.

My brother Shanmugam and his wife Mala with their children Priya, Ahila, Son-in-law Raj and their grandson Kushan

That was the kind of money- lender my father had been!!

There were several signed promissory notes from many of his close and well known friends who had borrowed from him but most of them claimed when we checked with them later that they had either settled their loans without taking back their promissory notes or were unable to settle as they were in financial difficulties. Only God knows the truth?? But the few, who had given their deposits to my father, were all waiting eagerly to collect their deposits from me. That's life!

My family lawyer, Mr. Paramjothy had executed a will under my father's name when he was seriously ill in the hospital and had named my sister Sarojini and me as the executors of his will. We realised very soon that there was hardly any properties or money for us to claim in order to execute my father's will except an amount of RM 30,000 which was due from his former housing development partner Mr. Rethinam Chettier who readily agreed to settle the money without us executing my father's will. The shocking discovery that I made among my father's documents were several insurance policies worth several hundreds of thousands of ringgit but had all expired before my father had passed away. My father had no money even to pay for his insurance premiums. That was the state of his financial situation!

As days moved on and from the discovery I made about my family's financial condition, I realised the

My youngest brother Arumugam and his wife Ratha with their children Nadia, Narain and Anna.

Family get together (standing) My mother Neelambal, my younger sister Lakshmi (sitting) my sister Saro's mother-in-law Madam Visalatchi, sister Saro, niece Gayathri and my late brother-in-law Jambulingam

32, Jalan Segget, Johor Bharu where it all began for my family. My late grandfather started his first retail business in 1932, when it was known as Rengasamy Chettiar & Sons.

burden on me was really tough and I will need to sacrifice all my personal dreams including acting in movies for the sake of my family.

Among the many problems I faced was one pertaining to my uncle Kandasamy's family. The love and respect that my uncle Kandasamy had shown to my father as his elder brother had never wavered throughout his life and my father had been over-protective of his younger brother never letting him go on his own despite the fact that he had his own family and life. My aunty Chandra had been a good housewife. After her marriage to my uncle, she lived jointly with our family and had quietly raised her five children. In the bargain she had also taken equal responsibility in managing the kitchen and cooking along with my mother for our families and the hundreds of guests who had come to my house since her marriage in1961. But realising that her husband was not being allowed to go on his own to manage his family and to show his capabilities, she had always wanted her husband and her family to go on their own but had not been a possibility while my father was alive.

Trip to Genting with my sister Lakshmi, her late husband Sivanesan, my wife Renu and my 2 eldest children Ashwini and Thulasi

She approached me one day, explained to me her feelings and situation and requested me to allow her family to go on their own on my return from India after completing my housemanship. I realised that what she was requesting was reasonable and promised to fulfil on my return. Needless to say, it was not an easy task when it really happened!!

I realised I had to complete my housemanship and return soon to resolve all my family problems that was plenty and pending. I wanted to settle my family finances to keep my family going before I left for India. I also had a pending debt to Mr. R. Balakrishnan

My sister Lakshmi and her daughter Vetharubini

Overseas family trips: With Renu and my three children Ashwini, Tulasi and Nadesh

of RTM who had paid for my father's entire funeral expenses.

Among the many Hindu beliefs, one is that the family is duty bound to pay for their parents' funeral expenses. When I approached Mr. Bala to repay the amount that he had spent on my father's funeral, what he told me really touched my heart. He declared my late father had been one of his closest friends and mentor in his life. He owed to him for all the good lessons he had learnt in his life from my father and that he had always been grateful to him. He further added that what he had done for my father was a personal thing between two close friends and that I should not attempt to settle the money if I really respected him and his friendship with my father. Despite my appeals to him to allow me to settle the debt, he refused to accept. How many of us are lucky to have friends like Mr. Bala in our lives? I will never forget my respect for his kindness even though he is no more. I still remain a close friend of his family. I did get back an opportunity in later part of my life to pay

back his kindness in some form and I am grateful to God for that.

Having been in Malaysia for about a month, I had to leave for India to complete my houseman-ship and another huge task which was waiting for me. The division of our family properties in India had to be administered between the Malaysian and Indian families for which I had to take the relevant power of attorneys from both my family members and from my uncles' Mr. Kandasamy and Mr. Subramaniam, the eldest son of my step grandmother who was in Malaysia.

My sister Sarojini agreed to take charge of the family affairs till I returned. She has always remained a loving, capable and responsible sister to all of us till now.

On my return to India, I reported back for duty to my professor Dr. Collin who was kind enough not to have given me an extension of my posting. I have always remained grateful to her kind consideration.

The run down shophouse at 3 Jalan Tun Abdul Razak in JB(formerly Jalan Wong Ah Fook) where i was born on 4 th August 1950. This was where my grandfather established his spice grinding business in 1933 and was well managed by my late grandmother Madam Valliammal who provided the seed money when my grandfather Rengasamy Chettiar ventured into both his provision and spice businesses.

Partition Of Properties

Having resumed duty, I had to now look into the affairs of our joint family's property partition in our village. While most of the properties had been acquired through the hard work of my late grandfather and my father, the properties had never been divided even after my grandfather had passed away in 1964. Though my father as his eldest son had the responsibility to divide the properties which consisted of more than 150 acres of both wet and dry agricultural lands and a bungalow, he had never shown an interest to partition the family properties.Father left everything to his step mother and her children to manage which later turned out to be a wrong decision. My grandmother though capable had to rely on her second son Rajamanickam to help her manage the properties and the agriculture business that the family was dependent on for their income. Her two other sons Dorai and Arumugam were still young and they were not decision makers in the family business.

With Rajamanickam despite being a kind person was not made out for business and was only interested in whiling away his time with a musical and drama troupe that he was heavily funding.

Rajamanickam's lack of interest in agriculture, the family's cultivation business went down forcing them to borrow heavily and selling several of the hard earned lands on defaulting on their loan borrowings from the government and private individuals. This had been going on unabated since my grandfather passed away and my father had allowed my step grandma to handle without supervision or check and balance. On my part, I had never ever questioned my grandmother or my uncle Rajamanickam either on the family's earnings or properties in the village except for the occasional pocket monies I used to receive from my grandmother while my father was alive. More than that, it was also because I was loved both by my grandmother and uncles. There was never a reason to question them. In fact, the question of family partition came about only after my father passed away when the urgency of wanting to save whatever was left of our family's wealth arrived. Less than 75 acres from the original 150 acres my grandfather had acquired remained. My uncle Subramaniam, who was the eldest son of my step grandmother and a timid person did not have a good and cordial relationship with his other siblings and had in fact requested me to look into this grave financial situation before I left for Malaysia.He wanted me to resolve it urgently on behalf of the family in order to save whatever that was left and for which he had given me his absolute power of attorney.

I was hesitant at first to broach on the subject of the family partition issue with my grandmother in case it created any misunderstanding. Fortunately, they all readily agreed.

As my grandfather never left a will, I had to turn to the good office of the 'village panchayat' or village committee which is the usual practice in India to help out in our family partition. We had no more common landed properties in Malaysia to share with the family partition except for the two premises in Johor Bahru from which we were receiving rental income as chief tenants. I could have demanded for an equal share in the properties both for my uncle Kandasamy and myself but to be fair to my step grandmother and her children I did not.

Except for six acres of agricultural land and two empty plots for housing for both my uncle Kandasamy and my family, I agreed to give everything else including the family house to my grandmother and her sons. What could have been an easy family partition turned out to be an isssue because of the ruckus created by my youngest uncle Arumugam. He became argumentative and refused to agree to settle all the outstanding loans that had been taken by his elder brother Rajamanickam on behalf of the family blaming his brother squarely for the mismanagement and for the losses in the family business. Not only that, he also refused to give a share to my uncle Kandasamy accusing him of not contributing anything to the family's wealth. I refused and told him bluntly that there will not be any family partition if my uncle Kandasamy was left out. There were also verbal abuses between Rajamanickam and Arumugam despite the appeals from the village panchayat members.

Thereafter despite my regular visits to my village to reconvene the meeting to settle the issue, my uncle Arumugam continued to play hide and seek avoiding and refusing to come to a settlement till much later after I had left the country. Matters

became more difficult for all of them because of the huge loans and debts the family had.

The final job of getting the family partition settled fell on my younger brother Venugopal who was still in India then. He got another round of fresh power of attorneys from my uncle Kandasamy, Subramaniam and my own family members. With the family partition done successfully, all that remained between our Malaysian and Indian families was only the blood ties.

A few years later, my uncle Subramaniam whom I had represented as his power of attorney decided to sue his stepbrother Kandasamy and me for a claim against our family's rental income that we were deriving as chief tenants from our two shop houses in Johor Bahru!!

With my father's death still lingering in my mind I kept away from social activities and gatherings except to concentrate on my houseman postings and to spend time with my friends privately. I kept regularly in touch with my sister Sarojini on our family affairs.

My second brother Shanmugam had in the meantime arrived in Chennai to pursue his higher studies. But after trying for a seat for a while to pursue his studies, he decided to return home to Malaysia to get involved in business where his interest really was.

Wedding on 9th April 1978

Renu Comes Into My Life

It was November and Deepavali, the Hindu festival of lights was around the corner. But the usual custom was we do not normally celebrate any festivals for a year if we had lost a close member of our family. I was invited by uncle Jayapal and a few Malaysian friends to join them for Deepavali lunch and dinner. As I was lonely, I decided to join them not realising for a moment that I would be meeting one of the most important persons in my life there, Ranuga Devy or Renu for short. There she was sitting with another good friend, Lily. She was simple and casual, wearing broad glasses. She was from S.I.E.T College and had first seen me in 1973 performing on stage singing the Baila during OSA show to raise funds for the Chief Minister's Relief fund. She belonged to a group of girls in S.I.E.T. who never had a good opinion of me and believed I was more of a Casanova in town!

While I was in the house, she was avoiding me and never made eye contact with me. I was mystified by her behaviour and decided to have a go for her more so out of curiosity rather than interest. All of

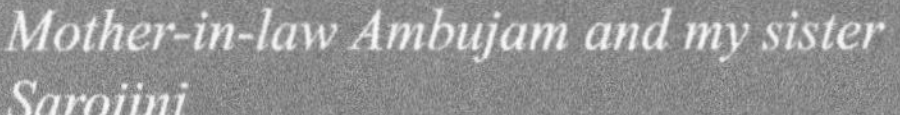

Mother-in-law Ambujam and my sister Sarojini

Renu with her grandparents late Mr. Nadesan and Madam Packiam, Cousin Kasturi

my friends decided later in the evening to celebrate Deepavali at the then famous and popular Taj Coromandel Hotel disco.

The girls were all dressed for the evening and I saw Renu looking extremely beautiful amongst them!! During the dance session, I invited her to dance more than others and I could notice a tinge of fear in her eyes and her strange body language despite her attempt to indulge in a brave conversation with me. I made a play for her, teasing her in the bargain. In the midst of our conversation our discussion turned towards the late President John Kennedy and the year he was killed. I said he was killed in 1963 whereas she was arguing saying that it was in 1964. I told her it was a bet and that she should go out on a date with me if I was right. She agreed and lost the bet but she stood me up on our first date out of fear of going out with me. I made it a point to complain to her friends Lily and Anne. She must have heard that I complained. She then agreed to go out with me later, more so out of fear for me.

Our first date was a simple outing for lunch. She obviously was on her edge and worried whether I would do anything to her with the kind of reputation I was supposed to have. Well, she must have been surprised and relieved that nothing went wrong on our first date. To me, she was a simple girl compared to all the fun loving out going girls, I had been going out with.

Initially, I was only interested in her companionship but as days went by, we started becoming close especially after our outtings.

We spent many days together and enjoyed the outings. I was really sceptical at first of my feelings towards her. I was surprised that I was taken up by Renu as it was not intended to be!!! It must have been her simple ways and unassuming nature that must have attracted me towards her. She must have also realised that whatever she had heard about my wayward ways from others could not be really true!! As our relationship grew she had even written to her grandfather who brought her up from birth to get his consent to go out regularly with me?? This may sound funny but that was the truth!!!

It was December 1975, I was just about completing my second houseman posting when my friend VT. Rajan, a leading film distributor in Malaysia introduced me to a Mrs. Devy Maniam from Singapore. She was a show promoter and was in the midst of organising a series of stage shows in conjunction with Ponggal festival in Singapore and Malaysia in January 1976 with a group of cinema artists led by a leading film actor Srikanth. She was facing some difficulties in getting the travel visas cleared for the artists from the Reserve Bank and VT Rajan had requested my help in this matter as he knew that I was friendly with the Reserve Bank Governor. I agreed and helped to clear the visas which impressed Devy Maniam very much that she extended an invitation free of cost to me to travel with the artists to Singapore and Malaysia for the shows.

As it was four months since my father had passed away, I thought it would be a good opportunity to visit my family again.

Engagement ceremony - Dec. 1977

We left in the second week of January 1976 for the shows. The group was led by Srikanth and consisted of the following:

1. YG Mahendran a leading comedian and his wife Sudha. They were just married and it was sort of a honeymoon trip as well for them.

2. An upcoming actress 'Padafat' Jeyaletchumy and Kumari Padmini a leading actress then.

3. Actors Typist Gopu and Junior Baliah, the son of actor T.S.Baliah the famous doyen of Tamil film.

4. Brinda, a famous dance choreographer in Tamil films and her dancers.

A band from Singapore was arranged to accompany the group in their ten shows in Singapore and Malaysia. The first show kicked off in Singapore on Pongal day January 15th. It was well attended and the show went off well. I performed my famous Baila numbers on stage with the actors and actresses dancing which became a hit among the audience.

The second show was in Johor Bahru and it was organised by the JB MIC branch led by my late father for many years. The committee had decided to organise the show to raise money for a scholarship fund to be named after my late father. The show was successful and I performed on stage for the first time in Johor Bahru with my Baila numbers much to the delight of the Johor Bahru audience. I believe a fairly good amount was raised

from the show but much to our disappointment later, we realised that the scholarship fund in the name of my late father did not materialize for whatever reasons best known to the organisers.

I did not accompany the group except for two more shows in Kuala Lumpur and Ipoh, spending the rest of the time with my family and attending to matters that needed my attention. The whole trip was joyful and I became close to the artists, especially Srikanth. YG Mahendran and his wife have both remained close to me till now. I came to realise after spending time with the artists that while the film world was full of glamour and excitement, the personal lives of the artistes were totally different, true to the words that cinema was a celluloid world!!

my wife Renu being called to the BAR at the High Court of Johor Bharu with our family and her friend Mala Anton

We returned after two weeks and kept in touch with each other as we had become close to one another. Among the artists Padafat Jeyaletchumy turned out to be a very simple person belying the notion that artists are proud and arrogant. Misfortune struck her fame and stardom and she committed suicide a few years later. Suicides among film actors are very common as their lives are very stressful and competitive! I was glad I did not pursue my desire to become an actor.

When I completed my houseman ship in May, suddenly the seven years I spent in India seemed to come to an end. I had to say goodbye to the country that not only equipped me with life's lessons but made me a professional. It was an emotional departure.

Late Dato K.Pathma and his wife Late Datin Prema at our wedding reception held on 9th April 1978 at my recidence. s

At a book release function organised by me for former Penang MIC Chaiman Dato Subbiah's in Johor Bharu under Late Dato Pathma (Left to Right) Lawyer Venkadesan, Dato Subbiah, Lawyer Arunasalam Standing on Pathma's left Late Subramaniam, the temple secretary.

My Medical Career and involvement in public life

Dato K.Pathmanaban

On arrival in Malaysia, I registered with Malaysian Medical Council and thanks to Dato Pathmanaban who was the then Deputy Minister of Health, I was posted as a houseman in Johor Bahru, my hometown, to be near my family. I had to repeat my houseman ship in Malaysia a requirement then. The houseman ship turned out to be a very tough period unlike in India where there were so many of us manning a department.

My first posting was in surgery under Mr. Bhattal, a Sikh and a good human being. I had a good company of doctors who later became my personal friends to work with, like the late Dr. Harry Nanda who later became a general practitioner, Dr. Siow, a Japanese trained surgeon who later became a private specialist and had his own private hospital and Dr.Yahya Awang who became one of the most famous cardiac surgeons in the country and helped to establish the first Heart Institute in Malaysia. There were only six of us houseman manning the entire surgical department and we had to do several 24 hour calls in a month. That was the

Poet Vairamuthu's book release in Johor Bharu under Athi Kumanan where an amount of RM25,000 raised by me for Malaysian Tamil Writers Association building fund.

norm those days and with a monthly salary of only RM 650. It was harrowing to be a houseman. After all doctors are meant to serve humanity without expecting much monetary rewards!! It is a noble profession that saves lives. Should the doctor have any expectations? The hospital was filled with many Indian doctors especially housemen who had their education in India. Many of them like Dr. Joe Manuel, Dr. Theson, and Dr. Wilfred John became good friends and we worked well together as a group.

Despite my heavy schedule as a houseman, as in India, I became active again in many social organisations and bodies. I was elected to be the Chairman of the housemen committee of Johor Bahru, where I played a prominent role in the nationwide work-to-rule organised by housemen that was initiated to fight for better pay and working conditions. We succeeded in raising the pay from RM650 to RM1,240 after nearly 30 years much to our joy. Many of us were lucky to get back - pay as arrears. The best part of our struggle was it all started in Johor Bahru hospital when the then Health Minister Datuk Doctor Lee Siok Yew during a dialogue session with the housemen had mentioned by the slip of his tongue that he sympathized with us on our existing pay and that his driver was drawing a better salary than us. This led to an uproar among the housemen and we were rather shocked and surprised when a Malay lady houseman Dr. Latifah stood up and demanded that the Minister resign since his driver was earning better than the doctors. The Minister apologised for the low pay structure and promised to take up the matter with the cabinet especially the Prime Minister. This pay revision did materialise on 1st January 1977 but only after we went on the work-to -rule agitation that made the government take up this issue on a serious note.

In 1976, a group of enthusiastic Tamil friends of my late father decided to revive the Johor Bahru Tamil Association that had been so vibrant under my father but had become defunct since 1973 due to internal conflict among the committee members. The late A. Doraisamy, a Tamil school teacher, who had served under my late father in the Tamil Association (he was also my first Tamil

Tamilnadu former Speaker Tamilkudimagan's book release in Johor Bharu under YB Arumugam the then Johor EXCO Member on the right of Tamilkudimagan is the famous lawyer Subra Naiker.

Tan Sri Yahya, Cardiac Surgen who was my medical officer when i was a housemen in Johor Bharu General Hospital, 1976

Dato' Lee Siok Yiew, Minister of Health in 1976

Late Pathmanaban who became Swami Kuhabakthanatha, the President of Divine Life Society Malaysia

tuition teacher) initiated the move to revive the association and requested me to become the Chairman in the footsteps of my late father. Initially I refused to take up the position as I felt that I had family responsibilities and commitments but relented subsequently because of Mr. Doraisamy's persistence and supported by other members. I gathered a team of young Tamils to serve as committee members. When the news spread that the Johor Tamil Association was being revived and that I could be the Chairman, I was rather shocked by the opposition raised by certain quarters especially some of my close friends who were committee members of the MIC Johor Bahru branch. What is more! My late father had been the Chairman for a very long period in the same branch. Their argument was, instead of reviving the Tamil association I should join the Johor Bahru MIC branch as a member to serve the public. I explained to them that I was not interested in politics as I was bitter from my late father's experience in politics and that I was only interested in social service and work. Though they accepted my explanation they were not fully satisfied.

Book release of Lyricist Palanibarathi from Chennai under my chairmanship of Thendayuthabani Temple in Johor Bharu with Rajendran President of Malaysian Tamil Writers Association

Nevertheless, having taken up the position as Chairman I set about creating several social activities one among them being the revival of the Tamil section in the public library of Johor Bahru thanks to the then Johor Bahru council President. We decided that the Tamilar Thirunal festival should be revived. When the name of Dato G. Pasamanickam who was the then MIC state chairman and state Exco member was proposed as the chief guest by some of the committee members, they were pleasantly surprised and a little shocked that I did not object to their proposal due to the strained and acrimonious relationship my late father had with him in politics.

Though by then I knew what my father had gone through with his relationship with Dato Pasamanickam in politics, I felt that for the good of the society I should not harbour any ill feelings towards him who was then the state MIC chairman and also a state Exco member representing the Indian community.

We had the Tamilar Thirunal celebrations on 14th January 1977 on Pongal day with a series of cultural events culminating with a grand musical show. It was at this show that Manimaran who became a famous singer and entertainer in the years to come had his first stage performance. The show was a great hit with more than 800 people in attendance. It was also the stage where I made my first public speech in Tamil much to the appreciation of those present. Dato Pasamanickam gave a great and impressive speech in Tamil and appreciated the efforts we had put in to make the celebrations a grand success. It was also the first time I heard Dato Pasamanickam's speech and I was very impressed with his command of Tamil and his style of speaking!!

I decided that to be in public life the command of languages and the style of speaking was essential.

For three years I led the Tamil association carrying out several social activities till I was asked to take over as the Chairman of Thendayuthapani temple, where both my late father and grandfather had been chairmen previously, by the then secretary Mr. Pathmanaban who later became Swami Guhabakthananda and President of the Devine life society of Malaysia. When he spoke to me about becoming President of the temple I was very reluctant at first due to the fact I was too young to become President of a temple with no strong

As the Chairman of Johor Bharu housemen committee of the Johor Bharu General Hospital with fellow housemen.

religious background and still enjoying some of the habits that a temple President should not have.

Mr. Pathmanaban took a lot of pain in explaining to me that every individual is born with a particular talent and while he was studying to be a swamiji in life, people like me were also needed in carrying out our social obligations in the development of our society. He further explained to me the long history of the Thendayuthapani temple including the roles played by my late father and grandfather in the development of the temple. He also related the financial and other problems that the temple has faced in the recent years before my father had passed away and how the temple had been taken over by the official assignee of the government for management before some of the temple trustees the most prominent among them being Mr. Muthukumaru (known as a banker due to his employment with HS Bank) and a few devotees had applied for reregistration of the temple. It had been a difficult and long legal process involving Mr.

Subbarayalu Naidu the son of the late Mr. Perumal Naidu, the donor of the temple land, which had not been officially transferred into the name of the temple. Mr. Subbarayalu as the official administrator of his late father's estate was refusing to transfer the land to the temple demanding certain privileges in the temple for his late father like special pooja in the name of his father to be conducted daily and for him to be appointed as the new ad hoc committee President. It was only after the ad hoc committee members had agreed to some of his demands that he transferred the land legally to the temple much to the relief of everyone.

He was elected to the committee as the President of at the first AGM held in 1978. As he was giving and creating several problems to the other committee members in the management of the temple, it was at this stage that Mr. Pathmanaban, the secretary of the temple spoke to me about taking over as the new President in the next AGM to be held in 1979.

My Political Mentors

Tan Sri Subra's Family: Wife Puan Sri Suganthi, eldest Son Anand, second Son Datuk Sunther and the youngest daughter Datin Dr.Priya

Dato K. Pathma's Family: Wife Datin Prema, Eldest son Dr. Praveen (standing), Second Son Prashanth, Youngest son Pramokh,

Tan Sri S. Subramaniam and Dato K. Pathmanaban played pivotal roles as my mentors during the formative stages of my political career. Their guidance and wisdom served as invaluable compasses, steering me through the intricate world of politics. Under their mentorship, I gained insights into effective leadership, governance, and the art of diplomacy, which have undoubtedly shaped my political journey and decision-making processes. The lessons and principles instilled by these eminent figures continue to serve as a source of inspiration and guidance as I navigate the dynamic and complex realm of politics.

Tan Sri Subra began as a friend during my college days in India. Over time, our friendship deepened into a strong familial and political connection. I always held great admiration for his patience and the way he conducted himself with both his friends and political supporters.

As for Dato K. Pathma, he left a lasting impression on me with his remarkable intellectual knowledge, boundless patience, and unwavering kindness. He was a man of great honor, and his influence on my life and political journey was immeasurable.

The new Arulmigu Thendayuthapani temple of Johor Bharu built at a cost of RM3.5 million under my chairmanship. The kumbabishegam was held in 1999 under the auspicious of Swami Kuhabaktananda, President of Divine Life Society who was my secretary of Thendayuthapani Temple when i became the President 1978

Journey of Devotion
Our Involvement with
Thendayuthapani Temple in Johor Baru

The old appearance of Thendayuthapani Temple in Johor Bharu

Taking over as President of the Arulmigu Thendayuthapani Temple, Johor Baru in 1979 came with heavy responsibilities and hard work during the next 27 years till we completed a new temple in 1999 at a cost of RM 3.5 million and I gracefully retired as President in 2004 handing over the reins to my Vice President Dr. Vatumalai.

Several projects and improvements were undertaken for and behalf of the temple prior to the completion of the new temple. In 1980, we had to build a new temple office block with rooms for the accommodation of the staff at a cost of RM 50,000 as the old office was dilapidated and was in a collapsible stage.

In 1981, we purchased an adjacent land next to the temple from Devine Life society of Johor Bahru for a sum of RM 70,000 and had to put up a simple multipurpose hall at a cost of RM 90,000 for weddings and other functions being held in the temple to derive income. A special thanks must be

Laying of foundation stone for the New Thendayuthapani Temple under the auspicious of Tan Sri Kenneth Eswaran who donated RM500,000 for the construction of the temple, in the presence of Tan Sri Pasamanikkam

Raised an amount of RM250,000 for KPJ Investment fund and presented it to Dato Sri Samy Vellu in 1985 in which Dato Balakrishnan, MIC State Secretary being honoured. Seated is Dato S. Subramaniam, Deputy President of MIC

given to Divine Life Society who sold us the land that they had bought very recently at their cost price.

Thaipusam function, the main religious function of this temple for the last sixty years was drawing in huge crowds and the old temple was unable to accommodate them. A decision was made to build a new temple by purchasing a vacant land next to the multipurpose hall.

Our temple finance was in a very bad state of affairs when I had taken over, and we had completed the earlier projects through the kind donations given by our devotees, generous donors and by grants given by our elected representatives and the state government of Johor.

To purchase the land and to build a new temple seemed an impossible task at that point of time but nevertheless we embarked on it in 1984 with proper planning and trust in the Almighty and generous nature of our devotees, friends, donors and the general public.

Several innovative methods and functions were held in the next 15 years to raise the estimated RM 250,000 for the purchase of the land and another

At Vairamuthu's book release in Johor Bharu in which RM25,000 was raised by me for the Malaysian Tamil Writers Association (L-R) Athi Kumanan, Vairamuthu, Tan Sri Kenneth Eswaran, Dato S.Balakrishnan and writer Elanchelvan

At the Kumbabishegam of Thendayuthabani Temple in 1999 in which Datin Sri Indrani Samyvellu is felicitating my mother Madam Neelambal

RM 3.5 million for the construction of the new temple. The single highest amount of RM one million was raised through a fund raising dinner held in February 1999 well attended by more than 1200 guests including donors, prominent business and political personalities. One among them was Datuk K. Eswaran (who became Tan Sri later) a prominent businessman and a staunch devotee of Lord Murugan in our temple. He made a single personal donation of RM 500,000 towards the construction of new temple

Construction of the new temple was launched in 1997 with Mr. K. Dasen an engineer (who has since passed away) as the building committee chairman. He was a dedicated, honest soul and with the all round support from the devotees, committee members and the state government of Johor. Kumbabishagam or consecration ceremony was held successfully in November 1999, well attended by more than 5000 devotees. Of all the invited guests present, I was particularly very honoured by the presence of Swamy Guhabaktananda, the President of Divine Life Society of Malaysia. Pathmanaban made the construction of a new temple possible. I am convinced that of the many projects that I had undertaken and completed during the last 45 years in public life, the most

satisfying and gratifying was my involvement in this temple.

During my tenure as President not only did we promote Tamil language classes including the release of more than 50 Tamil books by different authors, we also promoted the ancient martial arts of Silambam and several cultural activities among the youth.

I have been particularly blessed by the good lord Murugan to be involved in this temple and to serve not only in religious activities but also in the promotion of language, culture and sports.

Having known the hardships and the financial disaster that my late father had encountered in politics, I was determined not to enter politics but like they say, fate had other plans for me!!

At a felicitation function for Tan Sri Doraisingam, Datuk B. Sahadevan and I by Malaysia Bharathi Tamil Mandram led by its President R. Thiagarajan and his committee members.

At the 50th Birthday celebration of Dato Sri Samy Vellu at his residence in 1986 together with MIC Bukit Chagar Branch members, from Johor Bharu

The Game Of Politics

In 1977, Samyvelu one of the Vice Presidents of MIC and Subramaniam, the then Secretary General of MIC contested for the post of Deputy President. I was invited by Subra whom I had known since 1974 to go on the campaign trail with him in Johor despite the fact that I was neither a member nor a delegate of MIC. I believe Subra knew that many of the branch chairmen and delegates from Johor still had lots of respect and love for my late father and my presence with him would be an added advantage to his campaign. I realised during the campaign trail with Subra the amount of respect my late father had commanded among the MIC members and branch Chairman. Despite strong support from delegates and leaders especially for Tan Sri Manickavasagam, the President of MIC, Subra lost by 26 votes to Samyvelu in the contest. This was made possible by support that Samyvelu commanded among the grassroots MIC leaders and Tamil school teachers who formed a substantial number among the delegates. Certain state leaders like Pasamanickam threw their support behind Samyvelu despite having given their word to Tan Sri Manicka that they would support Subra in the contest.

This led to further division in MIC especially among the leaders who were aligned to Tan Sri Manickavasagam, the President and Samyvelu, the Deputy President.

At Malaysian Diravidar Association function in Cha'ah, Johor under K. Pathmanaban, (L-R) Govindan Nair, Cha'ah MIC Secretary, YB Muthusamy, Batu Anam Assemblyman, Thiruchudar K.R. Ramasamy, President of Malaysian Diravidar Association and Dato K. Pathma

My involvement in politics started after this contest when several of my late father's well wishers who had formed the MIC Bukit Chager branch had cajoled and convinced me to become the Chairman to serve the Indian community. I had no great ambitions or desires to become a leading politician when I accepted the Chairman's post.

MIC Bukit Chager branch was officially opened by Dato G. Pasamanickam, the state Chairman in late 1977, I was determined to do my best for the Malaysian Indian community through politics. I was elected as one of the five states MIC Exco members in 1979 at the Johor state MIC conference against the wishes of Pasamanickam who had his own line up of five official candidates. It was evident to me then that he was not prepared to accept me into his fold as a team member in MIC despite the cordial relationship that I had with him for the last three years and knowing well his true colours.

In the General elections held in 1978, Datuk Pasamanickam who was the sole MIC representative in the state legislative assembly and state Exco was dropped as a candidate by Tan Sri Manickavasagam. This was the price Datuk Pasamanickam had to pay for having clearly supported Samy Vellu for the Deputy Presidents post in MIC against his promise to Tan Sri Manickavasagam to support Subra.

Before IPF meeting discussion being held between Thamizhmani, Dato M.G. Pandithan, Lawyer Subra Naicker, Standing Mohideen

At MIC General Assembly in Johor Bharu with Dato Govindaraj, Dato Pasamanickam

The nominated candidate was Muthusamy the state secretary of MIC Johor. Despite the attempts by Pasamanickam to exert his influence on the then state Chief Minister Tan Sri Othman Sa'ad, his personal friend, Tan Sri Manicka stood firm in his decision to replace him. This led to further division in MIC especially between the factions led by Samy Vellu and Subra, who had the backing of Tan Sri Manicka. Pasamanickam never forgave Tan Sri Manicka or Subra both of whom he thought were responsible for dropping him as a candidate. Muthusamy won the election but MIC paid a heavy price when the Chief Minister refused to nominate Muthusamy to a state Exco post, showing his displeasure against the dropping of his good friend Pasamanickam as a candidate. This feud continued

both into the State MIC elections and National elections in 1979.

Never did I realise that I would be facing my first test in politics in 1979 when a few committee members of my branch were instigated by the state MIC leadership to oppose me in the branch elections all because of my strong support to Tan Sri Manicka and Subra. There was also an impression that Subra would recontest Samy Vellu in the forthcoming MIC assembly for the Deputy President's post again in 1979.

I won the branch Chairman's post again uncontested but when the opposing faction led by my former Vice chairman K.G. Raman failed to win the Vice chairman's post they created a ruckus to disrupt

NLFCS Dinner function at Kluang to felicitate Tan Sri K.R. Soma and Puan Sri Soma on the award of Tan Sriship under the chairmanship of Lawyer Dato P.Venkadesan along with my wife Renuga, Datin Venkadesan and Kalaramu MC

Tan Sri G. Vadivelu

H.L. Tennakoon

the AGM and to declare it null and void. It did not materialise. K.G. Raman and his group took a legal suit against me and my committee to declare our elections invalid. This did not happen due to the clever handling of the suit by my lawyers Mr. Tennakoon and Mr. G. Vadivelu (later Datuk and Tan sri) an expert MIC constitutional lawyer.

The expected MIC re-contest between Samyvelu and Subra did not materialise despite Tan Sri Manicka's desire to have Subra recontest in the election. When Subra refused to contest, Manicka

tried to convince Pathmanathan the other Deputy Minister and his loyal supporter to contest. Pathma though very popular in MIC knew his limitation as he was a Malayalee whereas Samyvelu was a Tamil, the dominant faction in MIC. It was a wise decision by Subra not to contest since he had lost his Damansara parliament seat in 1978 general elections whereas Samyvelu had won his Sungai Siput parliament seat and had become a Deputy Minister in place of Subra. Mohandaskumar, a MIC leader from Penang and close friend of Subra had initiated a secret meeting in Singapore between Samyvelu and Subra till then arch political enemies to resolve their political differences. At that meeting Subra had agreed not to contest Samyvelu for the Deputy President's post and in return Samyvelu had agreed to support both Subra and Pathmanathan for two of the three Vice President posts in MIC. The elections at the MIC general assembly in 1979 went well and as expected Samyvelu won the Deputy President's post uncontested with Subra and Pathma winning the top two Vice President posts. Pasamanickam was the surprise winner of the third Vice President's post! Tan Sri Manicka

At Thendayuthabani temple function in Johor Bharu with RTM Sugumaran and N.S. Subramaniam. Seated is Lawyer P. Venkadesan

who was visibly upset with Subra for not contesting against Samyvelu refused to nominate Subra again as Secretary General, a post he had held for the last six years and instead appointed Mahalingam (later Datuk and Tan Sri) as the new Secretary General of MIC.

Immediately after the MIC General Assembly in 1979, a tragic event took place in MIC, which changed the course of history in MIC for the next 32 years!!

Tan Sri Manickavasagam the sixth President of MIC suddenly passed away from heart attack paving the way for Datuk Samyvelu to become the acting President of MIC.

Raised an amount of RM250,000 for KPJ Investment fund and presented it to Dato Sri Samy Vellu in 1985. Seated is Dato Pasamanickam, Dato Seri Samy Vellu, Dato S. Subramaniam

Silence was not My Option

Dato Seri S.Samy Vellu, President of MIC having lunch at my residence in Johor Bharu in 1985 together with Dato S.Subramaniam, Deputy President of MIC

This was the beginning of a new era which led to the opening of old wounds causing on and off turmoils and controversies in MIC for the next 32 years of Samyvelu's leadership in MIC.

On becoming the acting President of MIC, Samyvelu, his associates and supporters went on a witch hunt against supporters of Subra and Pathma with several state and branch leaders associated with them facing pressure and problems leading to change of their leadership.

These problems ultimately led to the convening of MIC central committee meeting on 26th May 1981, to expel Subra and Pandithan who had been an ardent supporter of Samyvelu for many years but had switched his allegiance to Subra and Pathma after being defeated in the 1979 MIC Vice Presidential elections for which he blamed Samyvelu squarely for not supporting him.

On that fateful day with more than 10,000 of our supporters surrounding the MIC building where the MIC CWC meeting was being held, in a sudden twist of event, Samyvelu who was on a warpath with Subra during the past years made a brilliant political decision to make peace with Subra after a 15 -minute private discussion with him paving the way for peace to prevail in MIC from 1981 till 1987, the golden era of MIC.

This action of Samyvelu was a master political stroke. Having realised that he only had 50 percent control of MIC, he knew very well that to implement his several projects and plans in MIC, he had to draw in the other 50 percent support which was with Subra, Pathma and Pandithan. What a brilliant scheme it was to make peace with his ardent political foes to make his ends meet!!

Datuk Samyvelu and Datuk Subra were elected unopposed as the President and Deputy President of MIC at the national assembly held in 1981 in Penang. Like wise Datuk Pathma, Pandithan and S. Govindaraj, a close friend and ardent supporter of

Samyvelu were elected as the three vice Presidents with incumbent Datuk Pasamanickam being defeated.

In recognition of this new found Peace and Unity in MIC, I handed over the balance of RM 15,000 out of the Rm 50,000 I had collected for one of the members of my Bukit Chagar branch who had a heart problem. We gave her RM 15,000 that was needed for her follow up after a successful operation in UK(patients were sent to overseas for heart operations at that time)and gave a further RM 20,000 to four other deserving heart patients.

I had handed over the balance of RM 15,000 to MIC National with the explicit understanding that a National Heart Fund would be created for deserving heart patients in the future which was never to be!! Another wasted effort of my MIC Bukit Chagar Branch and I!!!

One of my strongest supporter and friend V.Segaran

Several of my close friends who stood with me in all my struggles in politics.

The Death Of An Institution

At the election campaign of Dato Seri Samy Vellu in Sungai Siput in 1995

The time was right for Datuk Samyvelu to unveil his future plans for MIC starting with the purchase of Vanto academy an educational institute.

A nationwide donation drive was initiated in 1981 throughout the country through the MIC branches and my Bukit Chager branch contributed the largest single donation of RM 50,000 through a dinner function held in Johor Bahru. Vanto had a good reputation, name and success when it was managed by its previous owners. When it was taken over by MIC, several internal conflicts and interference by board members into the management led to a lot of confusion during the next few years leading to its closure after nearly 10 years. Greed for power and money killed the instituition.

This single largest contribution coming immediately after having contributed RM 15,000 to initiate a national heart fund for MIC members at the National Assembly caught the attention of the MIC branch leaders and National leadership especially Datuk Samyvelu. All of these contributions by my branch not only initiated my recognition in MIC but also led to my election to the central working committee. For the first time in 1984, I had the highest votes among several other contestant leaders like Datuk V.L. Kandan and Tan Sri K.S. Nijhar!! This came as a pleasant surprise to many.

MIC leaders especially branch delegates had already taken note of me and had been impressed with my Tamil speeches made during the general assemblies held during the past 7 years. This was because they did not expect an English educated medical professional to speak fluently in Tamil.

MAIKA Holdings

Tan sri Gnanalingam

In the next few years Datuk Samyvelu launched several other projects on behalf of MIC.

He launched Maika Holdings in 1985 to serve as an economic vehicle for the betterment of the Malaysian Indian community. An impressive RM 108 million was collected within a span of six months especially when there was an ongoing recession in the country. All sectors of the Indian community took up shares in MAIKA holding believing that this could be the turning point in the economy of the community. But alas it was not to be. After several business ventures failed the company folded up after 24 years. It was quickly taken up by a private group led by Tan sri Gnanalingam a prominent Malaysian businessman. This shattered the dreams of more than 60,000 shareholders who had believed in MIC when they invested their hard earned and borrowed money. Many lost their money when the banks that had provided loans to purchase the shares foreclosed due to default payments.

When Maika Holdings was launched, my branch committee members and I went on an intensive drive to raise more than one million in shares especially from our members and friends. I organised most of the collection single handedly. This again turned out to be the single largest collection among all the MIC branches in the country. I had taken a special effort since I had been elected with the highest votes in the Central Working Committee election and I wanted to prove my worth to the delegates who had placed their trust in me.

In 1985, after the successful launch and collection in Maika holdings, Datuk Samyvelu the Chairman of Koperasi Pekerja Jaya initiated an Investment fund to launch several housing projects throughout the country. My branch and I showed our mettle in collecting an amount of RM 250,000 in shares again the single largest collection among all MIC branches. This amount was presented to Datuk Samyvelu in a major function attended by more than 1000 members and guests.

Deputy Minister YB Saraswathy Kandasmy who played an active role during the MAIKA holdings turmoil.

On a overseas trip with Dato S. Subramaniam and Lawyer Retnasamy from Penang.

Political Promises Turn Theatrical

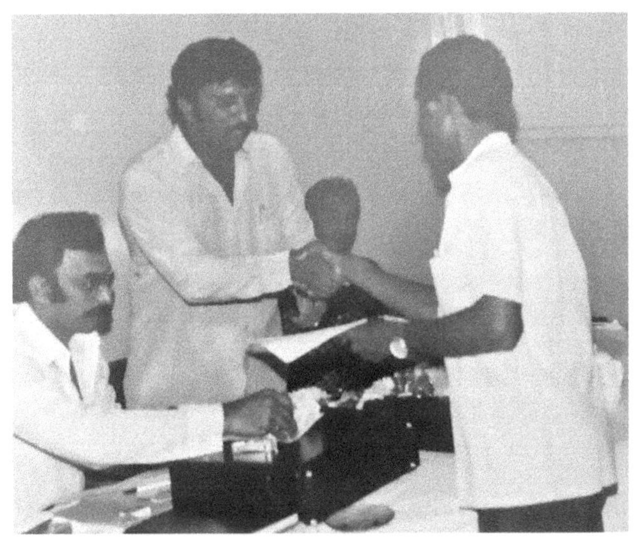

Datuk Samyvelu was so impressed with my performance especially after having received only RM 200,000 in an earlier function organised by the state MIC., he openly declared that I was the most preferred and potential MIC candidate in the forthcoming general elections in 1986 much to the joy of my supporters but to the shock and agony of the state leaders present who were hoping to be candidates themselves!!

In 1986, before the impending General Elections, Samyvelu as President conducted interviews with potential candidates after a central working committee meeting. I was one of those called and happened to be the last. It was around midnight and I walked into his room. He was looking exhausted and solemn. When I sat down, he started speaking.

'Dr Baskaran, I am extremely sorry, while you have done excellent work in MIC and you are one of the best potential candidates for the forthcoming general elections, the Johor MIC leadership especially the chairman, Dato Pasamanickam is

Courtesy call on Tan Sri Muhyiddin Yassin with my Thendayuthapani temple committee at his residence in 1986

extremely opposed to your candidature.' His words shocked me since the central working committee had given him an absolute mandate to choose and name the MIC candidates for the forthcoming general elections. But his following words comforted me. 'Don't worry Baskaran, while they (Johor MIC leadership) can only oppose your candidature in Johor, they cannot stop me for nominating you for a parliament seat in any other state or from nominating you to the senate.

He held my hand and said, 'I promise you, you will be nominated as a parliamentary candidate or as a Senator.' He appeared to be genuine in his promise at that time and there was nothing suspicious for me to doubt him.

In 1986, two months before the expected elections a new development unfolded. MG Pandithan, one of the Vice Presidents and an appointed Senator got into some serious political misunderstanding with Samyvelu. Pandithan who had been touted as a parliamentary candidate in the forthcoming elections was now considered a non- starter and in his place my name was being touted as a potential candidate.

The day before the MIC CWC was conveyed to announce the candidates, Datuk Kumaran, the Perak MIC State Chairman had been informed by Datuk Samyvelu during late evening that he was dropping Pandithan as a candidate for the Tapah parliament seat and in his place I may be considered as a candidate.

Datuk Subra heard the news from Datuk Kumaran. As I was staying with Datuk Subra, he conveyed this happy news. Surprisingly, just after midnight, Datuk Kumaran called Datuk Subra again to convey the news that Datuk Samyvelu had changed his mind and was nominating Pandithan as the parliamentary candidate for Tapah. This came as a shock to both Datuk Subra and I but nevertheless we accepted the decision, as Pandithan was part of our team. What had transpired during that few hours nobody knew till we found out much later that Datin Indrani Samyvelu had been the mediator and had arranged for Pandithan to meet with Datuk Samyvelu just before midnight in her house to apologise to him. That had brought an end to the feud between Datuk Samyvelu and Pandithan.

As I was not going to be announced as a candidate the next day, I took an early flight back to Johor Bahru. While I was flying back having accepted the sudden turn, another drama was unfolding in Datuk Subra's house the following morning. C.Krishnan one of the CWC members and a strong supporter of Subra had been considered as a potential candidate and had received a telegram from MIC Headquarters asking him to attend the candidates' announcement meeting.He was shocked when he was informed one day prior to the meeting by Mahalingam, the Secretary General of MIC, that the telegram was wrongly sent to him and he need not attend the meeting. Sivalingam utterly disappointed and frustrated took Krishnan, his close friend and strong supporter of Subra, to Subra's house to convey the news. Sivalingam pointed accusingly at Subra for not doing enough as their leader and deputy President to fight for his supporters to stand as candidates in the elections. Subra visibly upset and angry called Samyvelu on the phone to inform that he did not wish to be a candidate in the forthcoming elections and his Segamat parliamentary seat should be given to one of his supporters since none of them had been chosen as a candidate. Samyvelu was shocked (apparently) and pacified Subra by telling him to come to his office in the morning to discuss the matter to reach an amicable solution and decision.

I reached my home around 10 AM when I received a call from Subra who told me he had a discussion with Samyvelu that morning and that he had agreed to make an announcement and a press statement that three of Subra's allies namely Krishnan, Sankaralingam from Cameron Highlands and I as the next three MIC Senators in the scheduled afternoon meeting to announce the candidates for the general elections.

Dramas Within A Drama

Subra then told me to take the next available flight back to KL to attend that meeting. I dashed back to the airport to take the next flight back which was at 12 PM and reached MIC Headquarters for the CWC meeting just in time to hear Samyvelu making the announcement on the chosen candidates for the general elections. The three of us were announced as the next three senators as promised by him to Subra. The fourth Senator announced was Valli Muthusamy the MIC national women leader. I was happy that Samyvelu had kept his word to both Subra and me.

Having been announced as one of the future Senators, I played an active role in campaigning for the Barisan candidates especially for the MIC candidates in the 1986 general elections not realising for a moment that my role would be reversed in the next general elections in 1990!!

Barisan won with MIC scoring a 100 % victory for its candidates enhancing MIC and Samyvelu's reputation among the coalition partners.

MIC in good old days...

After the general elections when the time came for nominating four names for the post of Senators, another drama unfolded.

With MIC's 100% victory, there were numerous calls from the party members, congratulating the new senators. Subra's supporter, Sankaralingam was known to have a foul mouth and had an uncanny way of cracking dirty jokes especially about Samyvelu! His attitude and behaviour worsened the rift between Subra and Samyvelu.

Samyvelu, in one of the MIC meetings held in Morib had expressed his anger about Sankaralingam to Krishnan (one of the candidates for the senator's post), Sivalingam and Sankaran Gopal all of whom were identified as Subra's strong supporters. Samyvelu complained that Sangaralingam had been bad mouthing his family especially his wife, Datin Indrani and that he was definitely dropping him as candidate for a Senator's post. He further told them that he would accept anyone else to be recommended by Subra as the replacement candidate.

This outburst by Samyvelu created an idea in Sivalingam's mind. That he, having been a hard core supporter of Subra should be considered as the rightful replacement in the event Sankaralingam was being dropped as a candidate. Having consulted Krishnan and Sankarangopal both of whom supported him, they left immediately to meet Subra to convey to him what Samyvelu had just told them and to request him to support Sivalingam as the replacement candidate.

Unfortunately, Subra was not taken up by their suggestion and told them that Samyvelu should stick to the original four names including Sankaralingam that they had agreed upon.

Despite their pleadings especially by Sivalingam who had been very close to Subra including setting up Tamil Osai a Tamil vernacular daily with him in the early 80s to fight for his (Subra's) political struggle. Subra refused to change his decision.

This caused great anger and disappointment in Sivalingam who felt cheated by Subra. Another glaring factor was Subra and Sankaralingam were from the same Gounder caste and to Sivalingam who was from the Thevar caste this was another reason for Subra's refusal to drop Sankaralingam's candidature.

Sivalingam decided to go his own way to achieve his political ambition and to add fuel to fire was none other than G. Vadivelu, Subra's former long term close friend and political ally who had fallen out with him when he was defeated as Koperasi Nesa director in 1985. Fortunately, Krisnan and I were related to G. Vadivelu and we maintained our relationship.

Vadivelu who became a Datuk and Tan Sri later was a very shrewd politician and a good political lawyer. He had been a state assemblyman and a strong supporter of Tan Sri Manckavasagam and had been closely identified as one of the members of his inner circle together with Subra, Pathma, Kandan and Mahalingam. He had been handling several of the cases faced by MIC including my own case in my Bukit Chager branch in 1979 and was quite renowned for this. He was a well known political enemy of Samyvelu who despised him. All this changed because of the severe misunderstanding between Subra and him over the allocation of legal and conveyance cases for the Taman Nesa housing scheme in Scudai, Johor. He had been dominating the legal work in Koperasi Nesa for several years but when Subra as President of Nesa decided to split the conveyance legal work between Vadivelu and P. Vengadesan, another lawyer, a close friend and political ally of his in Johor Bahru, all hell broke loose.

Vadivelu was visibly upset and felt cheated by his long term friend. He was not prepared to share the cake with Vengadesan and started a smear campaign against Subra over this and other issues. He particularly highlighted the fact Subra and Vengdesan were from the same Gounder caste!! This infuriated Subra who changed his mind and awarded the entire conveyance legal work of Taman Nesa to Vengadesan driving the final nail down on his friendship with Vadivelu. In 1985.Vadivelu was defeated as a Koperasi Nesa director in the elections.

Vadivelu in his vengeance to teach Subra a lesson moved closer to Samyvelu his long term political enemy through the good offices of S. Palanivelu, the younger brother of Samyvelu who was his former student and had been close to him.

Dato Sivalingam

Tan Sri Mahalingam

Tan Sri Vadivelu

Into his hands fell Sivalingam who by this time had his own issue to grind with Subra. They decided to plan their political moves for their own benefits!! Joining them was Krishnan who was an easy prey. Krishnan had been a close friend of Sivalingam but a strong supporter of Subra. To convince him to change his political thinking came easy to Sivalingam and Vadivelu as the replacement candidate, Sivalingam together with Vadivelu as his political guru and Krishnan set in motion a grand plan for their political future!

Having been denied by Subra to recommend him for the Senator's post, Sivalingam decided to move forward with his own plans to secure the seat by meeting Dato Mahalingam the secretary general of MIC and the Selangor state MIC chairman who had distanced himself from Subra and Pathma. He had become closer to Samyvelu who had continued his appointment as Secretary general since he took over as acting President 1n 1981.

The Senate seat that was meant for Krishnan was from Selangor and had been vacated by Pandithan who had been nominated as a Parliamentary candidate in the 1986 elections. This was only a period of 15 months to serve out of the three years term. Sivalingam hit the right button by taking the issue to Mahalingam who was the Selangor state MIC chairman and told him how Subra was refusing to nominate him for the senate seat instead of Sankaralingam.

Mahalingam having realised the opportunity to break up Subra's group and to impress Samyvelu with his political manovering, he promised to speak to Samyvelu on this issue as Selangor state chairman. He invited Krishnan the other nominated candidate for Senate for a discussion. Mahalingam had become his relative due to Krishnan's second marriage to one of his relatives. He knew the weakness in Krishnan and frightened him by telling him the folly in accepting the 15 month- senate that will not give him any retirement benefits if he is not nominated for a second time. He further stressed as he was already a government servant he may lose even that retirement benefits

if he resigned abruptly to take up the 15- month Senate post. As Krishnan was already in a confused state, Mahalingam advised him to meet Samyvelu to explain his predicament and that he would also put in a good word for him to Samyvelu. Krishnan then met with Samyvelu who listened to his problem and promised to consider him for a full senate putting the nominations of the three others who had been promised full term senate seats in jeopardy. Mahalingam who had his own political plans to move up the MIC leadership hierarchy had by then convinced Samyvelu that it was the right time to breakup Subra's support and his inner circle by nominating Sivalingam to the Selangor senate seat and to nominate Krishnan for a full term Senate seat instead of Sankaralingam!! That was what I too believed till the last moment when another drama unfolded in Samyvelu's office on the day the nominations for the four Senators were being forwarded to the Prime Minister's office.

Samyvelu who had been expressing his anger about Sankaralingam's foul mouth to everyone, saw me during one of his visits to Johor Bahru for a meeting and told me to follow him in his car back to the airport. Tan Sri K.S. Nijhar, the then treasurer general came with us in the same car. Samyvelu expressed his anger against Sankaralingam and told me clearly that he was not going to nominate Sankaralingam even if Subra insisted. He made it clear that I was his number one candidate in his nominations and that he would nominate anyone else recommended by Subra except Sankaralingam.

I tried to pacify him by requesting him to speak to Subra on this matter but he remained adamant. This happened at the JB airport on a Saturday and in front of Tan Sri Nijhar who had been quite friendly with me and he told me not to pursue this matter about Sankaralingam's senate nomination anymore with Samyvelu. I then decided to lay off the issue but nevertheless, I told Subra what had transpired and how Samyvelu was adamant in not wanting to nominate Sankaralingam for a senate's post. I was grateful that Samyvelu still had me in his mind for the Senate's post till another bombshell fell on the following Monday.

There was an article in the Star newspaper on Monday written by Letchumanan a Star journalist close to Samyvelu. He had written about the four nominees for the four Senators' posts and had mentioned that I would be likely dropped as a nominee. This shocked me beyond words since Samyvelu had assured me just two days ago that I was his best and number one nominee. But since it was written by someone close to Samyvelu, I believed there could be some truth in the article. I immediately contacted Tan Sri Nijhar who was equally shocked by the news and was wondering what had gone wrong within the last two days since Samyvelu had confirmed my appointment. I then contacted Subra who told me he too was not aware about what had happened and told me to go and meet Samyvelu quickly to sort out the matter. I rang Samyvelu's office and was told he would be in the office on Tuesday. I took a flight the next day and went straight to his office in KL, where another political drama was waiting to unfold.

I walked into his office, sat down in front of him and asked him whether there was any truth in the Star article. I went on and told him the sacrifices I made to launch the various projects successfully for MIC. He gave me a hard look and said to me," Yes you have performed well in MIC but you are not my man. If there was a problem between Subra and me tomorrow, I know where your loyalty will be!!"

I pleaded with him saying I had looked upon him as my leader for the last 12 years and though Subra was my friend, I have never betrayed him in any matter. He agreed that I have been a devoted worker but my loyalty was always with Subra. He then threw a bomb shell. 'Your loyalty and friendship has been with Subra all these years but believe me you are not his number one nominee for the senate ship but Sankaralingam. What he really meant was, despite my friendship and loyalty to Subra, he was recommending Sankaralingam, a person who belonged to his own Gounder caste!! His words really shocked me for a moment, but I could not believe Subra would do this to me. I urged him saying since he is the President of MIC and had the mandate to nominate anyone for the Senate post, to nominate me on the merit of my work in the party during the last 12 years.

I never realised at that point of time that these were not the words that he wanted to hear from me. He would have been very pleased if I had condemned Subra when he revealed that Subra was canvassing for Sankaralingam. That was my first political mistake but I could not bring myself to do that betrayal since Subra had been my close friend for several years and my political mentor in politics.

I realised that was a fallacy and my fool hardiness many years later. Samyvelu then told me, he would give a serious thought to my nomination after meeting and discussing with Subra the following day. That was an absolute lie since I found out a few years later that he had forwarded the four names minus mine to the Prime Minister on the same day after I left his office and without meeting Subra the following day. But I also found out much later that Subra too had played an indirect role in this political drama where I was dropped as nominee for the Senator's post. The least expected Sankaralingam along with Krishnan and Valli Muthusamy were nominated for the three full term Senate positions while Sivalingam who left Subra to find his own political path was nominated through the Selangor Senate seat. This was the revival for a greater political fight in MIC.

My interaction with Malaysian political leaders

Sinister Manouvres

When I had told Subra that Samyvelu was adamant about dropping Sankaralingam as a nominee for the senate's post after my meeting with Samyvelu in JB, he had told this to Sankaralingam and had urged him to see Samyvelu quickly to settle his issues with him. Sankaralingam had immediately gone to see him in his house the following day to convince him that he was an innocent party and had not spoken ill about Samyvelu or his family especially about his wife Datin Indrani. He must have been a great actor to have convinced Samyvelu that he was an innocent and harmless person. This probably would have caused Samyvelu to change his mind but I believe there was more to this than the simple act by Sankaralingam for him to have changed his mind. He was a planner and had shown his mantle.

Firstly, he knew Sankaralingam was not a well- accepted politician in MIC. By nominating him he knew the Senate post would be wasted but he would not be a political force or threat whereas on the other hand if he had nominated me I would use the Senate position to do political work especially for Subra and Pathma and in the bargain we would become more popular in the party.

Secondly he had already broken Subra's close knit political group by driving a wedge between Subra and his close supporters Krishnan and Sivalingam by highlighting to them Subra's insistence in nominating the original three of his supporters especially Sankaralingam to the Senate positions which he did not oblige and neither kept to his original promise to Subra.

Thirdly he had denied me a Senate position and had checkmated both Subra and my ever -growing influence in the party. He had also hoped to break my friendship and relationship with Subra by dropping me as a candidate; Subra had indirectly dropped me as a Senate candidate by insisting on Sankaralingam's candidature though he knew Samyvelu was against him all the way. He also knew about Sankaralingam's inability to perform and do political work but had insisted on his nomination for whatever reason best known to him??

I was made a scapegoat in the on going political drama and shadow play between Samy and Subra. The gainers were Krishnan and Sivalingam who made the timely switch to cross over to Samyvelu where as I became the loser for refusing to do the same. Whether I made the right or wrong political decision at that point of time is something I would never be able to answer!!

Despite the fact that I was cheated of my nomination for a senate post, sympathy and support grew for me among the members and delegates of MIC. Many genuinely felt sorry for me for not being rewarded for all the handwork I had done in MIC and quite a few chided me for not being clever enough to play the right political drama with Samyvelu to convince him for my senate seat.

I came to know about the truth behind the senate drama a few years later from Sambanthan, the Executive secretary of MIC who had been sacked at that time. We met at a restaurant and he asked me what had gone wrong in Samyvelu's office on the day I had gone to see him about my senate seat. On that day when I left Samyvelu's office I had met Sambanthan outside his office. Sambanthan was a hardcore supporter of Samyvelu and Mahalingam and an unfriendly person especially to Subra and his supporters. On that particular day he had smiled and had shaken my hands when I had passed by him. He revealed to me at our meeting years later that he had brought a letter addressed to the Prime Minister with the four names including mine as nominees for the Senate posts as instructed by Samyvelu. But after I had left Samyvelu's office, he had come out from his room and had instructed his personal assistant to retype the letter to the Prime Minister leaving my name out and to include Sankaralingam's as the fourth nominee. He had been convinced after my discussion with him that despite telling me that Subra was more in favour of Sankaralingam rather than me for the Senate post, I had not been swayed by his disclosure and had remained steadfast in my conviction about Subra. This had irritated him and convinced him that I would not leave Subra and cross over to him even after he had given me the senate seat. This is the irony of politics and I was made a victim!!

Despite having been left out as a candidate for a Senate post, I came out with a thumping victory with the highest vote in the CWC elections a second time around in the party elections in 1987 but not before another interesting political drama had taken place prior to the elections.

Mahalingam who had his own political plans for his future managed to convince Samyvelu that Subra and Pathma's political influence was growing in MIC and that a check should be put in place by allowing him and two of Samyvelu's close supporters Dato Muthupalaniappan and Dato Pasamanickam to form a team to contest against Pathma and Pandithan in the Vice Presidential elections. They wanted to defeat them in order to reduce Subra's support in the party. To achieve this end, Mahalingam as Secretary General and with the blessings of Samyvelu had deliberately formed hundreds of new MIC branches in Selangor to increase the number of delegates from Selangor believing this would help him in his quest to defeat Pathma and Pandithan in the Vice Presidential race.

Mahalingam and the other two Datos together formed a formidable Datos' Team. Subra and Pathma knew they had to formulate their own strong team to defeat the powerful Dato Team and in this aspect they had to have a strong third candidate along with Pathma and Pandithan in the

interfere in the contests for the rest of the political posts. Without openly campaigning for their preferred candidates both Samyvelu and Subra campaigned subtly but strongly for their candidates especially in the Vice Presidential race.

All three of the Datos team members lost including Samyvelu's preferred candidate, Mahalingam. Even in the CWC elections only Tan Sri Nijar, a close supporter of Samyvelu won whilst the rest of the four winning candidates including me were close to Subra. These results shocked Samyvelu but it came as no surprise to delegates and party members. A wind of change had turned the direction of the party. Despite coercion, threats and money politics, majority of the delegates took a firm and strong decision in wanting to vote against all of Samyvelu's candidates. These results led to the re-emergence of political differences and turmoil in MIC between Samyvelu and Subra.

Vice Presidential race. Being popular in MIC, I was considered as the first choice by Pathma but Subra was against it saying that in his view only two of our candidate will win and the third winning candidate would be Mahalingam. Subra insisted I would win hands down in the CWC contest and should not be sacrificed. Pathma and Pandithan agreed with Subra's view. S.S. Subramaniam another prominent politician and a Samyvelu supporter who had been denied by Samyvelu to contest for the Vice President's post offered himself as the third candidate to Subra.

Samyvelu and Subra were elected unopposed as the President and Deputy President of MIC again in 1987 with a clear understanding that they would not

Having failed in their bid for the Vice Presidential posts the three datos began their vendetta by scheming against Subra, Pathma, Pandithan and their supporters. They made it clear to Samyvelu and convinced him that they had lost due to his waning support and control over the party and that Subra was already setting in motion his plans to

contest against him for the Presidential post in 1989. This was not true at that time, but the interference and false information given by Vadivelu, Sivalingam and Krishnan who had crossed over to Samyvelu further convinced him that they were telling the truth.

Vadivelu, Sivalingam and Krishnan began their own political manoeuvres to prove their loyalty to Samyvelu and to move into his inner circle. Sivalingam fired the first salvo by creating problems in the management of Tamil Osai a Tamil daily he had started together with Subra and with Athi Kumanan, a great Tamil writer and journalist as its editor way back in 1981. The paper had grown and had become the best loved Tamil daily with the highest circulation in Malaysia thanks to the several hard hitting articles written by Athi Kumanan over the several issues faced by the Malaysian Indian community. Many of the articles had pointed out the inefficient leadership provided by the Indian political parties and leaders, especially MIC and Samyvelu. These articles had irritated Samyvelu and had often created misunderstandings between Samyvelu and Subra on several occasions. It took Subra to personally appeal to Athi Kumanan on many occasions to be more subtle and moderate in his writings against Samyvelu and to maintain the peace in MIC. While Samyvelu had always suspected Subra was the majority shareholder of Tamil Osai, it was Sivalingam who confirmed this to Samyvelu.

With Vadivelu providing the legal brain, Sivalingam created enough damage to kill Tamil Osai that was eventually taken over by the government official assignee and saw its demise shortly. This was a major political setback for Subra and his supporters.

Tun Daim Zainuddin

Fortunately, Sikkander Batcha who was the permit holder and owner of another Tamil daily Malaysia Nanban came to the aid of Subra and Athi Kumanan by leasing his permit to them to initiate the publication of Malaysia Nanban as a Tamil daily which soon became the leading Tamil daily in Malaysia thanks again to Athi Kumanan's writings and articles.

Vadivelu meanwhile started writing several damaging articles against Koperasi Nesa of which Subra was the President culminating in a very damaging front page article in Tamil Nesan another Tamil daily which belonged to Samyvelu and his family. He created an impression that Koperasi Nesa was being mismanaged by Subra and its board of Directors and was soon going to be bankrupt. This created great panic amongst the shareholders and several hundred fix deposit holders. This panic caused a run of the money in Koperasi Nesa and brought their daily operations to a halt. All these actions of Vadivelu had the blessings of Samyvelu.

Koperasi Belia Maju Jaya of which Pathma was the President faced the same problems created by similar damaging articles in Tamil Nesan. These issues created by Vadivelu and Samyvelu had damaged both Koperasi Nesa and Koperasi Maju Jaya to a critical level that both Subra and Pathma had to urgently seek the help of both Dato Sri Dr. Mahathir, the Prime Minister and Tun Daim Zainuddin, the Finance Minister to intervene and settle several financial problems faced by both cooperatives headed by them.

The timely help rendered by both these leaders in bringing Bank Negara to intervene salvaged the future of both these cooperatives and its members.

The taking over of these two co- operatives by Bank Negara was timely and stopped the run of their funds but came with a heavy price. Many of the loan recipients and Directors were subjected to severe investigation to rule out any foul play and mismanagement by the board of directors of both these co -operatives.

I was a loan recipient of Koperasi Nesa having initiated a housing scheme on a 15 acres of prime land in Plentong, Johor some time in 1985. I had recruited about 40 house buyers who were Nesa share holders and had paid deposits amounting to about RM 200,000 as booking fees. With this amount in hand, I had arranged with Nesa to provide the balance of RM 450,000 as loan to pay the purchase price of RM 650,000. With my hands on method and through my close connection with the state government officials, I managed to get the approval for a housing scheme very quickly but unfortunately I was unable to start the construction as a bad recession was setting in Malaysia. The loan had to be serviced and I was unable to do so resulting in the loan ballooning to about Rm 800,000. By this time Nesa went into problems in 1987.

Just before Bank Negara stepped in, Nesa lawyers advised that it would be best for me to settle off the loan by surrendering the land to Nesa to square off my loan failing which Bank Negara with their immense and wide powers may take severe action against loan defaulters like me. At that point of time it sounded to me as sane and good advice, but that was the second time I had made the wrong decision. As part of my loan settlement with Nesa and without considering the financial implication, I had also undertaken to settle the deposit of Rm 200,000 which I had collected from the potential house buyers. I only realised the full potential and the real value of the land much later after I had surrendered it to Nesa!

With no elected position in the party and with my limited involvement in medical practice, I was beginning to face severe financial and several political problems. Despite being double crossed on several political promises, I pursued with Samyvelu to make him honour his promise to me especially after my overwhelming victory in the CWC elections in 1987. I had scored the highest votes the second time around and this time I doubled the 1984 votes of 666 votes to nearly 1100 votes. Yes, '666' the number of votes I had secured in 1984 and which I believe is associated with the 'devil' was probably the reason for my failure and downfall in MIC!

When the next senate vacancy fell, Samyvelu pulled his trick again. I was cheated of course! This time due to the vindictive efforts of both Mahalingam and Muthu Palaniappan who having lost in the Vice Presidential elections had convinced Samyvelu to appoint one of their closest supporter VK Sellappan from Selangor who was a Gounder but who also happened to be a strong supporter of Samyvelu. Just before the latest senate appointment was made, I had met Samyvelu in a party function and had appealed to him to honour his commitment to me. He moved closer to me, held both my arms and said to me, 'Dr Baskaran I feel sorry for you. You have become the victim of political circumstances'. After saying those words, he walked away and that would be the last time any nicety would exist between us. This was not the end of my politics but it came with more disappointments and miseries.

M.G. Pandithan with our supporters on the day he was expelled from MIC in 1988

The Hunt To Kill

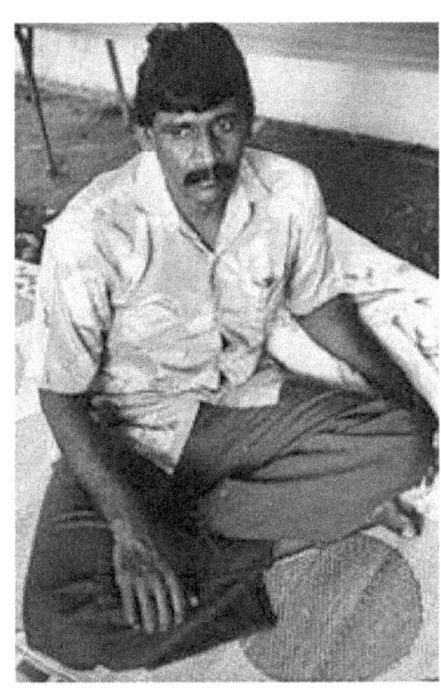

Having realised that they could not bring down Subra and Pathma through the issues they created for Nesa and Maju Jaya co operatives, Samyvelu and his political advisors began planning their next move.

In 1988, using a provision in the MIC constitution, they suspended more than 150 MIC branches that were supporting Subra and Pathma and which had failed to pay their annual branch quotas on time to obtain their B forms which allows them to conduct their annual general meetings as per the constitution and Registrar of societies requirements.

During the past six peaceful years in MIC, branches used to pay their quotas even after their due dates, obtain their B forms and have their AGMs. All this changed due to the fear created by Samyvelu's scheming cronies in the mind of Samyvelu that Subra and Pathma were planning his downfall!!

While these political problems were going on, Pandithan created another major issue in the party. Having won in the general elections in 1986,

Pandithan had been appointed as a parliamentary secretary that gave him the cloud to travel around the country. He was gradually strengthening his political support especially among the Dalit community the backward caste that he belonged to and other backward communities who were a dominant force in Malaysian Indian politics more so in MIC. This did not go unnoticed by Samyvelu and his advisors.

Samyvelu became irritated and had apparently started condemning Pandithan on many occasions about his role in playing the caste system in politics especially after he had won in the Vice Presidential elections the third time in 1987.

In a moment of anger and without giving due thought to the political consequences, Pandithan brought an empty 'coffin' to the MIC headquarters and announced that he would fast to his death till Samyvelu apologised for all the disparaging remarks he had been making against him and his Dalit caste. This action of Pandithan made headlines in the various media causing tremendous humiliation to Samyvelu and MIC. It also angered the majority of the Malaysian Indian community that had grave objection against the frivolous use of coffins for political games! Samyvelu did not need anymore reasons to go after Pandithan.His idea of protest back lashed him.

Having realised that Pandithan their closest political ally was caught in his own act and would spell death of his career in MIC politics both Subra and Pathma advised him to give up his fast, seek an urgent meeting with Samyvelu to explain and apologise to him. Pandithan reluctantly yielded and attempted to meet Samyvelu several times but was in vain. Ultimately he managed to meet him in London. According to Pandithan, Samyvelu had apparently listened to his explanation and had agreed to forgive him when he apologised. But Pandithan walked into the

hungry lion's den. SamyVelu and more so his political inner circle wanted to get rid of Pandithan, the strongest ally of Subra and Pathma. They then went for the political kill.

Pandithan was served a show cause notice by the MIC Disciplinary committee. This was what we call a 'Wayang kulit' show. The committee asked him to explain his action in bringing a coffin to the MIC headquarters. In their opinion it had caused irreparable damage and humiliation to MIC. Pandithan apologised for his rash behaviour but Samyvelu and his cronies had predetermined Pandithan's fate.

On the day of the CWC meeting there were more than 5000 supporters of Pandithan and us waiting outside the MIC headquarters while it took Samyvelu and the CWC members less than 10 minutes to discuss and decide on expelling Pandithan from the party. A well planned political drama had been staged within the short possible time to expel Pandithan, a senior Vice President. The shocking thing was Subra, Pathma, Masilamani, AT Rajah and me, the five CWC members who were in support of Pandithan walked in just ten minutes after the meeting had started at 9 am being shocked with the decision, requested for a review but it was turned down.

Samyvelu and his CWC supporters left immediately in their cars for fear of their safety since the crowd outside the building was growing in numbers but not before waving their hands to the waiting crowd hoodwinking them into thinking that Pandithan had been left scot free. When they realised it was not so after the five of us came out and spoke to them, all hell broke loose and there was pandemonium all around among the members and supporters present. Subra after having told me to stay back to prevent any untoward incidents among our supporters and to show support to Pandithan which was much against the wishes of Pathma, left with him. Masilamani and AT Rajah to plan their next move. Pathma feared that leaving me behind may create unnecessary problems for me in the future and what he predicted came true subsequently.

I did not realise at that point of time that I would become a political scapegoat and victim again although I was able to contain our supporters from doing any serious damage and harm to the MIC building and the MIC staff caught inside.

MIC was well prepared for this ugly scene and had brought in enough police personnel especially the tough Reserve unit to control the crowd. Despite their presence, the agitated and angry supporters with their emotions running high entered the MIC building compound belting with stones and attempting to burn the party flag. Their agitation was brought under control by the strong police force that arrested many of them. Meanwhile Pandithan having arrived with a huge entourage realised the political tragedy that had befallen him and made a fiery speech to his supporters urging them to fight against the tyranny and dictatorship of Samyvelu. I had stood there to show my support and sympathy for Pandithan that eventually led to my own expulsion from MIC just like Pathma had predicted.

They succeeded in expelling Pandithan from the party, which was part of a grandeur scheme to weaken the status of Subra and Pathma. This was plotted by Samyvelu's political advisors, his cronies and a new member Palanivelu, the press secretary of Samyvelu. They now turned their attention to Masilamani and me,the other two CWC members and strong supporters of Subra and Pathma.

Just like Pathma had anticipated, I received a show cause letter from the disciplinary committee of MIC headed by Dato Nijar asking me to explain why I was seen standing next to Pandithan on the day of his expulsion!! It was a stupid show cause letter, but that was the golden opportunity Samy Vellu would cash on!

Despite a lengthy and detailed explanation reply written by Pathma on my behalf and endorsed by Datuk Kandan, our team member and a prominent lawyer explaining that I was present there to prevent any untoward incident. I was still called by the Disciplinary committee to appear before them to explain my action.

Dato Nijar, the Chairman of the disciplinary committee prior to my appearance   revealed to me that the whole exercise was a farce!

Nevertheless, many of the CWC members and Samyvelu's supporters advised me to meet Samyvelu prior to the next CWC meeting to explain and apologise to him for my action. But by this time, I had become totally dejected, vexed and disappointed with Samy Vellu. I refused to listen to their advice.

As usual with several thousands of our supporters surrounding the MIC building and in the presence of hundreds of police personnel especially the Reserve unit, the CWC meeting was conducted. During the proceedings, I challenged Samyvelu to give me an opportunity to challenge him for the Presidents post to be held in 1989 to prove his

support in the MIC. Samyvelu in his usual style laughed at my suggestion and told me my fate will be decided by the CWC.

When the decision was announced by the CWC to expel me from MIC, there was an outcry and mayhem among our supporters gathered outside the MIC building and as usual the strong police and Reserve unit force present kept them at bay and under control.

To ensure that my challenge to Samyvelu for the MIC President ship was widely published in the Malaysian media, I delayed receiving my expulsion letter from MIC with the help of my postal friends. I called for a press conference in my house that was attended with much fervour by the various media to express the high handedness and atrocities by Samyvelu and his cronies in MIC and to announce my candidature against Samyvelu in the ensuing Presidential election in 1989.

My challenge to Samyvelu created wide publicity in the media but it only amounted to that. In early January 1989, I accepted my expulsion letter after ensuring that I had good publicity of my challenge to Samyvelu and turned to my good friend and a very prominent lawyer Subra Naicker for legal advice and further action.

Subra naicker had been a very strong supporter of Samyvelu and we never saw eye to eye till Subra naicker mounted a challenge against Pasamanickam for the Johor state MIC Chairmanship in 1984, for which I had been touted but had to withdraw at the

last minute due to Samyvelu's advice and insistence. Subsequently I contested in the CWC elections and won with the highest votes.

Subra Naicker decided to go for the post and made peace with me for my support. Though several others had given him false impression and hope that he could win including Gunapathy, an ardent supporter of Samyvelu but opposed to Pasamanickam. I clearly and honestly told him that he could not win and had in fact predicted that he should be happy if he received more than 51 votes based on my calculation. True enough, despite his aggressive campaign, he only received 51 votes. To add to his disappointment, prior to the elections at the state AGM, Samyvelu ran him down and spoke highly in support of Pasamanickam instead. This hurt had disappointed him severely causing him to break his ties with Samyvelu and to swear vengeance against him.

This break in his ties with Samyvelu brought him closer to Subra and Pathma but more so with me. We became close friends and decided to join hands, he with his monetary power and me with my grassroots support. It was a friendship that was never to be broken till his untimely death in 1989 but not before doing several political battles together. We decided that he would concentrate on state politics whilst I would concentrate on national politics.

He worked tirelessly and got an exparte injunction against my expulsion in 1989 which enabled me to participate in several of the on going state MIC Annual General Meetings, much to the anger and disappointment of Samyvelu. By then Subra Naicker had passed on and lawyer Ramasamy from Muar had taken over my case. Unfortunately, when my case came for full hearing at the Johor Bahru High court, my exparte injunction was removed and my expulsion from MIC was effected thus ending my 12 years of political career in MIC.

After expulsion, both Pandithan and I decided to form 'Narpani Manram' a Social conscious society and embarked on a nationwide tour from Johor Bahru to explain the atrocities and wrong doings that was going on in MIC under Samyvelu and his cronies. We planned a '100 -day meetings' held throughout the country. It was well organised by our supporters and drew thousands of members from MIC and the general public. We were cheered on by those present whenever we spoke about Samyvelu and the wrong doings that were going on in MIC and its projects especially in Maika Holdings which was established with the hard earned money from MIC members and the Malaysian Indian community. While Maika Holdings had been formed with lots of promises and hope to the Indian community, it was facing huge financial losses due to mismanagement and investment in nonviable projects.

In the Maika Holdings AGM in 1989 where I had gone with about 500 shareholders and supporters to question the Maika directors on its performance and financial situations, a well- conceived plan was in place to create chaos and to prevent us from questioning them. As planned, the tough looking rowdy elements organised by them and present in the hall began attacking us physically with the intention of causing bodily injuries especially to me when I started questioning DP Vijendran the Chairman and the rest of the board members on the performance and losses faced by Maika Holdings. I was truly lucky as I was saved from severe body injuries by my supporters especially one Paramasivan who personally protected and shielded me from the violent attacks. Imagine collecting one million shares for Maika when it was launched and now being personally targeted with physical violence at its AGM. What irony!!

The physical fight in the hall led to the arrest of many of our supporters by the police who in particular targeted our group. I had to personally go to the Dang Wangi police station to release all of my supporters who had been arrested by giving the police my personal bail and bond. This ruckus at Maika AGM was reported widely in the Malaysian Media much to the annoyance and displeasure of Samyvelu who was personally blamed for it for the unnecessary and inflammatory speech he had made at the AGM about Koperasi Nesa and Subra that was irrelevant at the Maika AGM.

While we were garnering support for Subra and Pathma we knew they would be the next political victims. Samyvelu's advisors were busy closing down another 150 of our supporting MIC branches in 1989 using the same constitutional provision

of non-payment of branch quotas on time. Subra and Pathma were partly to be blamed for this debacle. Having had the experience the previous year where 150 of their supporting branches had been closed on the same basis, they should have taken extra effort and care in ensuring their branches paid their annual quotas on time in 1989. This neglect on their part effectively closed down 300 supporting branches thus eroding their support in MIC just as Samyvelu and his advisors had planned.

While Subra had never intended to take on Samyvelu for the President's post in 1989, he stood at the cross road of his political career. By now many of his close team members and supporters had been expelled from MIC. Many thought he would not take on Samyvelu for the President's post but he took the crucial decision when he was left with no other option and after consulting Pathma, Pandithan, Masilamani, me and few of our close and strong supporters in a closed door meeting. When he announced his decision to contest at a large gathering organised by our supporters, I believe it came as a shock and surprise to Samyvelu and his advisors.

Despite the hard work put in by all of us and the huge support for Subra from MIC members and the Indian Community, he lost by a narrow margin as the voters for this Presidential election were only the committee members of MIC branches many of whom supported Samyvelu for their own personal and selfish gains. This was indeed shocking to Samyvelu and his supporters as he had used all his monetary and political powers to win by a big margin. There were many reasons for Subra's defeat, but one of the main being the withdrawal of support for him by Datuk Kumaran and Datuk Raju from Perak and their supporters who had consistently supported Subra and Pathma previously. They had their own reasons for doing this apart from their own political survival that they feared for knowing what Samyvelu was capable of doing if they had supported Subra.

With this defeat of Subra, we knew that Samyvelu and his cronies will go on a political vendetta against Subra, Pathma and the rest of our supporters in the party. Pandithan and I also knew this was the end of the road for our return to MIC and the doors would be permanently shut. Our political struggle

The stalwarts of Semangat 46 are Tan Sri Rais Yatim, Tengku Razaleigh Hamzah, and Ahmad Sabery

had to go on and our close friend and team mate Kanagasabai provided us with the platform when he offered to us to take over Indian Progressive Front a political party that he had registered and kept. We held several political meetings throughout the country that were well received and attended by the Indian community who by now had become disillusioned with the leadership of Samyvelu.

At this time UMNO too had been split due to the Presidential contest between Dr. Mahathir and Tengku Razaleigh Hamzah held in 1987 in which Tengku Razaleigh had lost by a very narrow margin. This had led to a court case in which UMNO was deregistered paving the way for the formation of UMNO baru by Dr. Mahathir and Semangat 46 by Tengku Razaliegh who was coordinating a huge opposition force and front against the ruling Barisan Nasional coalition to contest in the 1990 general elections. Tengku Razaliegh established the Gagasan Rakyat coalition which consisted of Semangat 46, PAS (a conservative Malay based party), Democratic Action Party and several other smaller political parties but without an effective Indian based party which was full filled by our Indian Progressive front after several discussions with Tengku Razalieh and Lim Kit Siang, the leader of DAP. We negotiated for four parliament and nine state seats for our party with Pandithan touted to contest the Teluk Intan and I the Nibong Tebal parliamentary seats.

When the general elections were called in November 1990, as expected Subra and Pathma were both dropped as parliamentary candidates by Samyvelu as the President of MIC. This created further anger amongst their supporters leading to much unrest in MIC.

The general elections in 1990 was a very tight and close elections for the Barisan Nasional as this was the first time since Independence a very strong opposition force had been established which was further strengthened by a sudden and unexpected turn of event when Pairin Kittingan the leader of Party Bersatu Sabah and Chief Minister of Sabah crossed over to Gagasan Rakyat from Barisan Nasional due to his differences with Mahathir with 14 parliament members who had won uncontested on nomination day thus creating a severe blow to the chances of a Barisan victory in the elections. While the whole country was abuzz with an opposition victory, the scheming ways of some of the Barisan leaders and the total control of media and government machinery thwarted an expected

opposition victory which was also contributed by the fear created in the minds of Malay Muslim Majority by the various media that the Christians were taking over the country since Pairin and several of the PBS leaders who had crossed over to the opposition were mainly Christians.

My own contest for the Nibong Tebal parliamentary seat in Penang taught me many new lessons in life. My contestant Dominic Puthuchery was not only a prominent lawyer and a leader of the Gerakan party that was part of the Barisan coalition and was in control of the Penang state government, he was also a known family friend who hailed from Johor Bahru, my home -town.

Penang was an affront state for our opposition group to capture in the 1990 elections as DAP was well established in Penang that had a Chinese majority. Lim Kit Siang the doyen of DAP had personally requested me to contest in Penang having known about my active political and public involvement. Nibong Tebal was totally a new place to me. Fortunately, Nibong Tebal was my old friend Mohandass Kumar's hometown. He offered his family house to me to be used as my campaign headquarters and residence during my election period.Mohan's manager,Subramaniam and his two nieces who stayed in the bungalow were trurly helpful to me during the entire campaign period and thereafter too.

When the nomination and election dates were announced I was totally worried as I did not have

Tan Sri Lim Kit Siang and the Late Karpal Singh the two DAP stalwarts who gave me a seat to contest in Nibong Tebal - 1990

any funds, having personally seen and known in the past many general elections how money was essential for a victory. With about RM 3000 given by my wife Renu in hand, I left to Kuala Lumpur with the hope that many of my well to do professional and rich friends would give me a helping hand. That was never to be!! Pathma while not financially well off gave me about RM 2500 which was the first donation that I received when I went to meet him to seek his blessings and wishes.

The election operation styles of Barisan and the Opposition differed when it came to political funding and spending. Funding was essential for all election candidates. In Barisan, most or all of the election expenses of the candidates are met by their respective parties and by Barisan in particular, quite apart from the donations given by their friends,

*Subra filing his nomination against Samy Vellu
for the MIC Presidential elections in 1989*

well wishers, political patrons and donors.

Political donations to Barisan, the ruling party for many years were huge, while the donations to the opposition parties were generally limited as there was not much of political patronage available in supporting opposition candidates.

With only RM 6000 in hand, I landed in Penang to file my nomination with the hope that I would receive some political funding from DAP quite apart from the donations I was hoping to receive from my friends and well wishers but it turned out to be a shock when I was told by DAP that I need to pay my own RM 5000 as my Parliamentary deposit! While some of my personal friends and family members helped but not the so- called rich professionals and business friends! It was my

grass root supporters who had stood and fought all along with me. They went around and collected some substantial amount of funds for me. I will never forget what I received from one of my schoolmates, a successful businessman. He helped me with a substantial donation with which I set forth with my election campaign but far below the amount any other candidate may spend.

To add to my financial burden was the fact that the Nibong Tebal parliamentary constituency was one of the largest constituencies in Penang encompassing three state assembly seats namely Jawi, Sungei Bakap and Sungei Acheh. The candidate for Jawi was from DAP and was a goldsmith whereas the candidate for Sungei Bakap was from Semangat 46 and a teacher. The candidate for Sungei Acheh was from PAS and was a taxi driver. Both of these last two candidates were not financially well off and I had to shoulder their financial burden as well when it came to bearing the expenses for our election campaigns.

As I knew Dominic Pudhuchery well and as we were both professionals we agreed to keep the elections clean and prevent any untoward or unpleasant incidents among our party members and supporters much to the happiness and relief of the local police and other authorities.

With the crossing over of Pairin Kittingan and his 14 members of parliament, the opposition front looked very formidable and appeared to be on its way for a great victory against Barisan Nasional

which was not to be. Apart from our limited election funds, Pandithan further worsened the situation by not fairly distributing the election funds he had received from Tengku Razaliegh. Barisan's total control of the various media helped them to use religion as fear factor to convince the majority of the Malay Muslim voters to change their minds at the last minute to vote against the opposition candidates.

The opposition lost narrowly in most of the seats in the general elections including losing in seven parliamentary seats by a total of 4000 votes which could have prevented Barisan from gaining the two thirds majority in parliament for the first time but it was not to be. My special thanks to K. Selvakumar, the late Gengan both from J.B., Mr & Mrs Thiagarajan (Muar) John Thomas, Sivaraj and a host of friends including Nadarajah(now a Dato) from Kedah,his brother Manoharan,Masilamani, Tamilmani and hundreds of grass root supporters who stood by me and helped me during the election campaign. God bless them all.

All of our IPF candidates, including Pandithan and I lost. My loss was the narrowest with just about 800 votes margin. I realised that this was the end of my political career having spent all my earnings and savings during the last 14 years in politics striving to be an honest, diligent and hardworking person.Several of the top IPF leaders including me, resigned from the party due to our major differences with Pandithan on the party finances he had refused to divulge till the end, including the

political funds received from Tengku Razaleigh.

Subra who was dropped as a candidate in the general elections by Samyvelu was brought back as a Deputy Minister through the timely intervention of Dr. Mahathir the Prime Minister who appointed him as a senator. Samyvelu despite the reluctance had to make peace with Subra for the third time around due to the insistence of Dr. Mahathir and reinstated him as the Deputy President of MIC again.Even at this stage Samyvelu played his political game when he tried to create a wedge between Subra and Pathma on the appointment of Deputy Minister, But Pathama true to his nature as a gentleman politician refused to fall into Samyvelu's trap.Thereafter the good human and politician Pathma retired from active politics to concentrate on his social and business activities. MIC thus lost a very intelligent and caring leader from doing more for its members and society at large.

This peace went on for the next 13 years till 2003 when there was another fallout between them. In 2004, Subra was again dropped as a parliamentary candidate due to his differences with Samyvelu. Subra contested for the Deputy President's post in 2006 but lost to Palanivelu who had the backing of Samyvelu, his political mentor. This led to Subra being dropped again as a candidate in the 2008 general elections which turned out to be the Waterloo for Barisan and for the first time lost their two thirds majority in parliament after being in power for more than 50 years. Several prominent Barisan leaders, many of them MIC leaders

including Samyvelu lost. SamyVelu was forced out of the cabinet after 27 years.

There was an attempt by some close friends of both Samyvelu and Subra to patch them up in 2008 after the elections but were unable to do so due to the differences between them in the Maika holdings issue. Subra lost again in 2009 to Palanivelu in the Deputy President election. Samyvelu finally stepped down as President of MIC in 2010 after having been in that position for the past 32 years thus paving the way for Palanivelu to become the 8th President of MIC. Subra never had a chance to contest again as he met with a serious medical problem which caused him to be bed ridden since 2011 thus ending his career in politics and public life. His ambition to become the President of MIC never materialised and ended as a dream for many

of his supporters. Datuk Subra who was bestowed with a Tan Sri award in 2012 while he was ill passed away peacefully in July 2022 thus ending his chequred career in politics and public life.

Datuk Pathma the highly respected gentleman and politician had been dropped as a candidate in the 1990 elections. He moved away from politics but maintained his ties with the Indian community and general public. He was highly regarded by Barisan leaders especially Dr. Mahathir the Prime Minister who appointed him as advisor to a few Government linked companies. Datuk Pathma who had been instrumental in setting up the Malacca Manipal medical college one of the first private medical colleges in Malaysia went on to concentrate in building up the college and in other business ventures till 2001 when he fell ill and passed away much to the sorrow and grief of his family, friends and the Indian community. He was an honest and dedicated politician and his passing away was regarded as a great loss to the Indian community and the country.

Pandithan having realised that he would not go far with the opposition alliance both politically and financially after the 1990 elections, switched his allegiance to Barisan Nasional for which he was rewarded with an appointment as a Senator for the

second time around and a Tan Sri award. Despite his switch of allegiance to Barisan Nasional, IPF was never admitted into the Barisan Coalition due to MIC and Samyvelu's continuous vehement objections. Though he made peace with Samyvelu after condemning him for several years, IPF was never admitted into Barisan even after the death of Pandithan in 2008.

With Subra being bedridden and with Pathma Pandithan, A.T.Rajah and Athikumanan having passed away a very important phase in the history of MIC and Indian politics in Malaysia had ended. From the original B team members, only Datuk Kandan, Masilamani, Nadarajah, Mathialagan and I are still around being active in our own ways less politics!!

All the other strong supporters have gone on to be active in MIC and other political parties while some have gone on to be involved in Non Governmental Organisations.

Datuk Kandan left active politics to concentrate on his prominent and successful law career. He became the Chairman of the well established and renowned Dr. Rama Subbiah Scholarship Fund after the death of Mr. R. Balakrishnan.

Dato Nadarajah who was active in MIC politics in Kedah has the distinction of being expelled twice from MIC for his support for Subramaniam and Pathma. He went on to do his law in London and also founded the MIC London club. He later joined People Progressive Party and became its Vice President. He subsequently left the party to concentrate on his law practice and his research on Bujang Valley on which he has written a very detailed book.

Mathialagan who was active in MIC politics in Perak, left to do his law and runs a very successful law practice in Ipoh. He leads the celebration of the yearly Thamizhar Thirunaal Festival in Perak. He writes regularly on Law in Makkal Osai Tamil Daily.

Masilamani left his position as a senior executive of Petronas to become a private consultant in education and training and was till last year the Chairman of Maju Jaya co operative that we had established in the 80s under the Chairmanship of the late Mr. Bala with Pathma as the President.

On my part, having realised the dire financial problems that I was faced with due to my involvement in politics, decided to concentrate on my family and business activities to redeem myself which was not easy to start all over again.

When I left politics at the age of 41 after 14 years not only had I lost my valuable youth and earnings of more than a million ringgit, I was also faced with a huge debt of RM 200,000 which was to be paid back to my depositors in my failed Plentong housing scheme.

A New Life

My involvement in politics also resulted in my selling five of my most profitable clinics to my partners leaving me with just two clinics. I went head long into my medical practice but realised that I would not be able to recoup my financial losses in politics nor repay my debts unless I was able to venture into other businesses apart from medical practice.

Though God did not grant me the two lifelong desires that I had nurtured to become an actor or a successful politician, I believe he has his own ways of rewarding those he wanted. I realised this when three business opportunities came to me in the next three years when I was struggling to pay my debts to my depositors in my housing scheme.

The first opportunity came in 1991 in the form of a Chinese buyer who wanted to purchase the Plentong land which he had assumed belonged to me when in actual fact I had already surrendered it to Koperasi Nesa to write off my loan with them before Bank Negara had stepped in to take over the management. I explained to him the full picture and told him about the debt I was owing to my depositors. To my surprise, instead of by passing me to go to Nesa directly to purchase the land, he agreed to appoint me to negotiate on his behalf to purchase the land within a price of RM 1 million and to let me make the difference of the purchase price as my fees. It took me more than six months of tough negotiation with Bank Buruh who were holding the land as a security for a loan extended to Nesa to agree to a sale price of RM 810,000 as a full settlement leaving me a balance of RM 190,000 to make as my fees. Having concluded the deal successfully, I was now worried whether the purchaser would pay me the balance as my fees since the land did not belong to me in the first place. But thank God the honest purchaser paid me as promised alleviating my problem to settle my depositors. This I believe was my first blessing from God for my honest and hard work in public life!!!

The second blessing from God came in the form of my friend Lim Chee Hong who was the CEO of a multi divested listed company in Singapore and had been introduced to me by Mr. Bala, my family friend. During one of his visits to JB in 1991, Lim had been impressed with the development going on in Johor and indicated to me that he would be interested in undertaking a housing development in JB if available. As I knew there were several empty lots that had not been developed by Nesa in their housing scheme at Scudai, about 15 kilometres away from JB and which was popular among the Indian community. I decided to approach Bank Negara which was in control of Nesa at that time to purchase them.

After a series of meetings, Bank Negara agreed to sell the 77 empty subdivided lots which consisted of 27 shop lots and 50 housing lots for a consideration of RM 3.5 million without any discount. The agreement between Lim and I was that I would act as a Director and consultant for the company undertaking the project with a

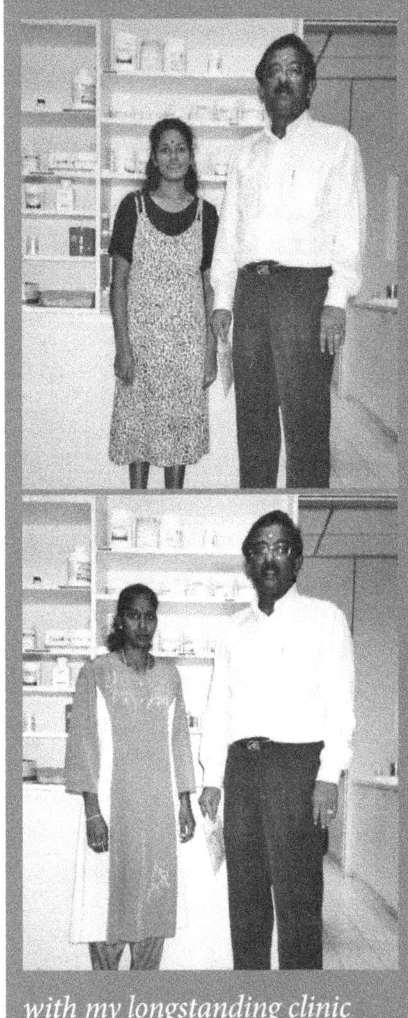

with my longstanding clinic nurses Parvathy and Thulasi who joined me when they were hardly 16 or 17 years old.

monthly consultancy fees and would be paid 20% of the profits if I helped to complete the project successfully. This was the break I was looking for and with the wide contacts that I had made during politics especially with the senior government servants and UMNO leaders in Johor including Tan Sri Muhiyuddin who was the Chief Minister then. I managed to get all the necessary approvals for the building plans and construction within a short period of time.

We decided to build the 27 shop lots first since there were none in the existing Nesa housing scheme. The shop lots were snapped up even before we had our official launch. I completed the construction way before the agreed period of construction time due to my easy ways and hands on method together with the timely help given to me by the various government departments and the officers whom I would never forget. The speedy completion and the successful sale of the 27 shop lots impressed Lim not only because we were able to settle the full bank loan that we had taken to purchase the 77 lots but it also left the company with substantial profits.

I now realised that the housing development ability that my late father had within him when he had completed his Taman Majidee housing scheme was in my blood too to an extent. Seeing my ability in handling the completion of the first phase of our development, Lim decided that we should turn the balance 50 remaining lots into a modern high rise condominium project rather than building them

into the housing units that they have been approved for. For this we had to first amalgamate the 50 subdivided lots. That was not difficult as I had good relationship with the government departments and officers. Unfortunately, this turned out to be a big mistake because when the approvals were given and when we were ready to launch the project in 1997 we were caught right in the midst of the worst Asian financial crisis.

If we had completed the 50 housing units as approved, we surely would have had a fire sale and would have come out successful with huge profits that would have benefitted me substantially. Having impressed Lim with my good work had caused me to lose huge sum in profits!!

My second blessing and business opportunity came to me in 1992, when another friend Philip Chan, whom I had known since 1985 when he had won the contract to build the 500 units of mixed development in Taman Nesa, Scudai in 1985, resurfaced and approached me with a joint venture proposal for a housing project with National Land Finance cooperative society or NLFCS, the largest Indian co operative in Malaysia on a 80 acres land belonging to the society in Semenyih, Selangor. Philip Chan had been introduced to us by one of our strong political supporters, Harikrishnan who was working for Philip in one of his housing projects in Kota Tinggi. When Philip won the Taman Nesa construction job on merit, he had obliged us by appointing Harikrishnan as his site

officer and had offered one or two subcontracts to our supporters. Though he did a good job in the beginning, he had faced severe financial difficulties towards the tail end of the construction and had failed to complete the job and as a result his contract was terminated by Bank Negara which had taken over the management of Nesa due to problems created by certain politicians and they had to appoint another contractor to complete the project Since 1979 most of Subra's supporters in Johor had stood by Tan Sri Somasundaram who had taken over the management of the co operative after the founder Tun Sambanthan passed away and was now opposed by Samyvelu who was keen for Mr.Loganathan, another director who was close to him to take over. The late M.K.Muthusamy who was the then assemblyman for Batu Anam and the MIC State secretary had stood with Tan Sri Somasundaram as a Director on NLFCS Board.

I had remained loyal and close to Tan Sri Somasundaram since then and even after Tan Sri Somasundaram had made up with Samyvelu in later years when one of his sons married Samyvelu's only daughter. Despite my political differences with Samyvelu I had maintained close relationship with Tan Sri Somasundaram that benefitted me when I approached him with Philip Chan's proposal since he was now in control of NLFCS.

Having known me for years and having seen me made a scapegoat in politics, Datuk Somasundaram was genuinely sympathetic towards me and helped me to secure the joint venture project between NLFCS and Philip Chan despite the fact that I was opposed to Samyvelu, his in law by then. He was my saviour at that time and I will always remember both he and the late Mr Vadivelu, the treasurer of NLFCS at that time who played an important role in getting the project for me.

I would also wish to express my gratitude to Datuk Sahadevan the present CEO of NLFCS and the then Senior Manager Late Mr. Srimalan who both helped me in securing the contract. Though Philip Chan offered to appoint me as the Chairman of his company with substantial shares, I declined and went on to sign a consultancy agreement with him for a fixed amount of fees for this and any other future projects that he may do with NLFCS and this turned out to be a wise decision.

Philip impressed Tan Sri Somasundaram and the board of NLFCS when he completed the housing project within two years rather than the five years that had been agreed upon and brought in substantial revenue to them from the first joint venture housing project that they had undertaken with a private third party. This led to Philip undertaking three more successful joint venture housing projects with NLFCS but unfortunately like the Taman Nesa housing project he was faced with severe financial difficulties due to the Asian Financial crisis in 1997 towards the completion of his third joint venture project with NLFCS.

Renu, Saro with her son Ayin, Mother Neelambal with my first born Ashwini, my second sister Lakshmi

Both these two projects with Lim Chee Hiong and Philip Chan was the turning point in my life and I was able to settle my outstanding debts and recoup all my substantial earnings that I had lost in politics. This was a true blessing from the good lord. With the new found prosperity and wealth, not only did I buy my first home in 1993 at Taman Bandar Baru Uda in Tampoi much to the happiness of my wife Renu but began investing in several other smaller properties and in other financial portfolios. The fear of having lost all my earnings in politics made me realise that I should not repeat the same mistake. My family life took a turn for the better and I was able to provide the necessities to my family that they had missed during my long involvement in politics.

My new found wealth not only gave me the opportunity to render financial help to my brothers and family members, it also paved the way for me to help all those real needy people who came to me for assistance. It gave me a new lease of life to get involved in various social and public organisations but never again into politics!! In particular, I turned headlong into the planning and construction of the New Thendayuthapani temple. I believe this was my duty and gratitude to Lord Muruga who guided me during one of my most difficult periods of my life.

During this period, seeing me handle the Taman Nesa shop house development effectively, Lim brought to me my third business opportunity in 1993. Mr Chang the chairman of his listed company had bought a five acres land some five years earlier near Saleng in Senai, Johor and tried several times to convert the land into a mixed development but without any success. Lim knew that with my good connections to the various government officials and politicians especially Tan sri Muhiyuddin the chief minister, I would be able to help in the project. With similar agreement as in the Taman Nesa project whereby I would be paid monthly consultancy fees to get the approvals and a 20% profit if the project was successful. I set about getting the necessary work done. As with the Taman Nesa project, I was able to get all the necessary approvals for a mixed development in the shortest possible time with the help of government officials and politicians. Like Taman Nesa second phase approval, the Saleng

Project approval too came right in the smack of the Asian Financial crisis of 1997 forcing us to abandon this project as well. If only both of these developments had taken place, I would have been a sure winner and would have ended up with several millions as my share of profits. God gives but he also knows when to stop?

Our listed parent company in Singapore had gone into severe financial difficulties due to the Asian Financial crisis of 1997 and had been placed under receivership by creditors. Lim had resigned as CEO prior to the financial problems faced by the company due to the interference of the children of Mr Chang, the chairman, into the affairs of the company. Prior to resigning from the company, Lim had warned me of the financial problems faced by company and advised me to exit taking my share of profits before the company was taken over by receivers. I did by taking over three shophoses in the Taman Nesa scheme in contra against my share of profits Despite my leaving the parent company, I worked closely with the new accountant and the receivers to help find buyers for the two abandoned projects in Johor. I even tried to get a few wealthy Indians whom I had known to invest and purchase the two valuable properties at much discounted prices but did not succeed.

With my son Nadesh Ganabaskaran on his being called to the BAR in London - 2009

Back Into The Folds Of My Family

While I was involved in politics and public life, I had some family obligations to fulfil.

Our family house was in a bad condition and needed urgent repairs. In 1977, with the repayment of RM 30,000 by Rethinam Chettiar, my father's business partner, I completed the urgent repairs with about RM 20, 000. The balance of RM 10, 000, I used to organise the wedding and reception of my eldest sister Sarojini who was a bank officer to Jambulingam, my school classmate and an accountant by profession. Both the wedding and reception took place on 31st August 1977 in Johor Bahru and were well attended by several well -known personalities including political leaders, family friends like Mr & Mrs Balakrishnan and Dr Anandaraman who had been our guardian to both my sister and me in Chennai. The good attendance at both these functions was overwhelming. My sister leads a peaceful and quiet life and has two children, Aiyinthiran a son, who is an Accountant like his father and a daughter, Gayathri, who has several degrees to her credit and now works in Melbourne as a co Ordinator of Community services. She is a true passionate social worker. Saro, my sister has been a pillar of support to all her siblings.

Immediately after my sister's wedding, I arranged for my uncle Mr. Kandasamy to be independent as has been a life long wish of my aunty Chandra in the presence of Dr. Anantharaman, as the mediator since he knew both of our families well. It was decided that my uncle would take over the Jalan Ah Fook shop of which we were the chief tenant and in addition I had to pay him RM 10,000 to move out from our home to set up his own house.

My younger brother Venugopal, came back from India after graduating and joined a private firm. Subsequently, he went on to do his own business. He married a pretty young lady Vasugi and has two daughters both of whom have graduated as professionals, the eldest Sankaree is an accountant and the youngest Kavitha, a lawyer. Both are happily married now. Sankary the eldest in happily married to Vigneswaran a fine young man and has

On the occassion of the marriage of my niece Kavitha in 2022 with family members

three children. The youngest Kavitha recently got married to Pradeep in 2022.

My second youngest brother Shanmugam was not interested in pursuing his higher studies but took keen interest in taking our family business in Kluang from Suppiah Chettiar who had been managing it for several years. I helped him to set up his career.

My brother was successful in managing our family business and was very supportive of me during my involvement in politics and public life. His helpful nature in over extending credit to his customers caused him dearly when the business started facing financial difficulties. A rather unfortunate accidental fire caused him to lose his business totally after which he turned to manpower business supplying local and foreign workers to local factories. He married a pleasant young lady Mala and has two graduate daughters Priya and Ahila. Priya is happily married to Raj from Chennai and has a son and are well settled in Malaysia. The youngest Ahila is a well known radio and television personality and is married to Sri Vignesh, a pilot.

My younger sister Thanalakshmi and my youngest brother Arumugam were both studying when I came back from India and I had to organise the additional funding apart from the amount that was given to them from our limited family income.

My sister Thanalakshmi, who has always been quiet became a Chartered secretary and joined a bank as an officer. She married Sivanesan a bank officer and has a daughter Vedarubini who has completed her degree in animation. Sivanesan passed away many years ago leaving my sister to care for her only daughter.

My youngest brother Arumugam completed his basic diploma in Engineering in Malaysia and left to the USA to complete his graduation in Masters in Business Administration for which we had to sponsor him. He started working as a store manager in a famous hypermarket, married Janet an American Filipino and settled down in USA.

My wife's second brother chandrakumar with his wife Kate and his daughters Monisha and Shona. They are settled in Sydney and have been the guardians and foster parents for my daughter Tulasi who is employed and settled there after her studies.

He has three children. Nadia, the eldest daughter, a son Narain and a third daughter Anna all of whom have graduated. Tragedy struck his wife Janet who went into a coma after delivering her third child Anna. She recovered miraculously from her coma and was declared a 'miracle mum' by the media only to pass away two years later due to breast cancer. To overcome the difficulty in raising his three motherless children, he remarried. Radha, his second wife who is a matured Indian lady and they have settled down in Houston in the USA. Both of them make great parents and business partners too.

My wife's youngest brother Jay kumar and his wife Manunmany who are very close and really helpful to my family.

Dato Dr.Raghupathy Naidu and Datin Dr. Krishna kumari. My wife's first cousin and his wife both of whom have always been closed to us.

A 'Kittangi Fellowship Lunch' initiated by our late friend Mr.N.Govindan for friends some 12 years ago was continued by our late RTM Mr.R.Bala. Now its being co ordinated by Mr.M.Arasu and Mr.M.Marren. Meeting every last Wednesday of the month, we have recently concluded the 120th lunch successfully.

Third Generation

My own family life began when I got married to Renu on 9th April 1978. She had come back from India in late 1977 after graduating with a Bachelor of Science degree in Nutrition. She did not look for a job immediately but spent her time with her grandparents and her uncle and aunty, Mr and Mrs Navaratnam in Ipoh where I visited her regularly. Their children Prakash, Ramesh and Anita became close to me as they are till today.

As Renu did not seem to be interested in a career, we decided to get married, as that was also the wish of her grandparents who were getting old. After having met her grandfather who gave his blessings, our engagement took place in December 1977 in Mr Nava's (now a Datuk) house in Ipoh that was well attended by our relatives and close friends.

Our wedding was fixed on 9th April 1978 and her grandfather was enthusiastically distributing our wedding cards when tragedy stuck just three weeks before our wedding. Her grandfather suddenly passed away due to a heart problem devastating Renu and her family members. While we were contemplating to postpone our wedding both our families decided to go ahead with our wedding since most of the preparations had been done and they did not want a postponement.

The wedding was conducted on 9th April 1978 as scheduled at the Johor Bahru Mariamman temple. Though we had intended to keep it at low key more than 1000 guests including VIPs consisting of political and business leaders attended our wedding since our wedding cards had been distributed well ahead of Renu's grandfather's sudden and unexpected death.

We settled with my mother in our family home since as expected of the eldest son. My mother and Renu got along very well, as Renu was keen to settle down as a home-maker rather than a career woman. She picked up cooking from my mum who is an excellent cook and turned out to be a good cook herself.

My eldest daughter Ashwini was born on 24th November 1979 much to the joy of the family. She was brought up by Renu and my mother who doted on her.

As our family life moved on, despite the small issues that cropped up between Renu and my mum which is typical in most families especially in Asian households, we stayed with my mum for the next 12 years. We had two more children Tulasi my second daughter, born on 24th June 1985 six years after Ashwini and my youngest son Nadesh, who was born on 19th May 1986.

Ashwini was a reserved child pampered for six years as our first -born. She was a very studious and hardworking student from the beginning. She completed her primary and secondary education with good results in Johor Bahru and pursued her tertiary education in Medicine at Malacca Manipal Medical college both in India and Malacca. She graduated well and worked first with government and subsequently as a General practitioner in Malaysia. She studied and got through her Fellow of the Royal Australian college of General Physicians degree. She met Ganesh an IT engineer in 2006 and got married on 9th March 2007. They have two lovely children, the eldest Janeesha a girl and the second Yashwin a boy. They migrated to Perth, Australia in 2013 and Ashwini has started her own General practice in 2016 after having worked with another medical group for two years. She is basically a family oriented person and minds her duties well.

My second daughter Tulasi was a bubbly child from the beginning. She used to display her multi talents in speaking, storytelling, and dancing in front of

our friends and relatives for which she was loved by all. She was not a hard working but an intelligent child when it came to studies. She got through both her primary and secondary education well in Johor Bahru and moved on to Sydney to complete her basic degree in commerce and a second degree in Chartered Accountancy. She worked in different fields and outfits and is now employed in a bank. A very caring person,who calls on us very often and visits us twice a year to keep abreast with happenings at home.

My youngest son Nadesh like most other boys was a playful prankster from the beginning. He was the favourite grandchild of my mum who hid most of his pranks from us but occasionally chided him. He did not display much interest in his studies during his primary education but became more concerned with his results during his secondary education since both his sisters were turning out good results. He completed his secondary education successfully and went on to study law in United Kingdom. He completed his law degree and Bar with good results. Came back to Malaysia, worked with a leading law firm for five years and went back to England to complete his Masters degree in Construction Law. He has started his own legal firm with other friends in Kuala Lumpur and is now practicing as a successful lawyer. He is the only one who is now around both Renu and me in Malaysia.

Though my political career did not take off successfully as I had expected, I believe I did not fail in my duties as a father and had completed my duties well and I deem the success of my children as my greatest success and fulfilment in my life.

While I am proud of the achievements of my three children, I am much prouder of the achievement of my wife Renu who despite taking care of my children during their formative years, while I was busy with politics, she fulfilled her own lifelong dream and ambition of becoming a lawyer.

I may have been the financial provider for my family but it was the sheer sacrifice and determination of Renu, my wife who saw through the excellent education, upbringing and success of my three children and at the same time achieving her own dream to become a lawyer. For that I salute her!!! She has now her own. legal firm and is also actively involved in the Malaysian Healthy Ageing society as an international speaker!!

All the above was made possible only because I had been forced to leave politics in 1990 and to focus on my business ventures and extend my duties and obligations to society.

The Chief Minister of Johor and my personal friend YAB Dato Khalid Nordin at the Annual Dinner of our Johor Cultural and Sports Club in 2017 where he gave the club an additional RM300,000 as grant from the Johor government apart from the earlier amount of RM1.2 million he had given to complete the Club House.

Committments And Fulfilment

With YAB Datuk Seri Ismail Sabri the 9th Prime Minister of Malaysia in 2004 when he was the then Minister of Sports. He was responsible for granting Silambam as an event in the SUKMA (Malaysian Games) games of 2008.

My ambition to complete the new Thendayuthapani temple in 1999 was successful.

I took upon myself to seek complete recognition for Silambam, the oldest martial arts in the world by bringing the sports into the Malaysian games organised by the Ministry of Sports in Malaysia every two years. In 2002, after having served as the Deputy President for several years I became the President of Malaysian Silambam Association founded in 1977. It was after approaching and impressing the importance of Silambam to four Ministers of Sports and more than ten Chief ministers from the various Malaysian states to make them understand the importance of Silambam it was included in the Malaysian games in 2008.

My special thanks to the following Ministers of Sports, Tan Sri Datuk Ghani Othman who gave Silambam its first recognition in the Ministry of Sports, Tan sri Muhiyuddin who gave us the chance to exhibit Silambam in the opening ceremony of

At the opening ceremony of JCSC New Club House on October 5th October 2013 with the then Chief Minister of Johor Dato Khalid Nordin, Tan Sri Sharir Abdul Samad, Former Minister and MP of Johor Bharu and Puan Sri Sharir

With the members of JCSC at the annual dinner in 2017

the Commonwealth games held in Malaysia. Datuk Hishamudin Hussein Onn, who gave Silambam the opportunity to be an exhibition game in the Malaysian games held in 2006 and finally to Datuk Ismail Sabery who gave the final approval to make Silambam to be included as a fully fledged sports in the Malaysian games held in 2008 Sukma. With this achievement I gave up the President's post in 2009 to pave the way for the younger leaders to take over the leadership of the Silambam association.

My next most difficult assignment and subsequent achievement came when I was urged to take over as the President of the Johor Cultural and Sports club which was formerly known as the Johor Civil Service club in 2002. This club founded in 1920 was the oldest club in Johor but unfortunately the club was in a bad state of affairs and financially no better when I took over as President.

As the club was placed centrally in Johor Bahru on a five -acre government land, it was considered very valuable by both the state government and private developers. It had been a leasehold land since 1920 but the lease had not been renewed by the state government since 1983 for whatever reasons best known to them. When I became the President I received the first shocking news when I received

At the opening of the new club house of JCSC on 5th october 2013 by then chief minister of Johor YAB Dato Khalid Nordin

a letter from the City council asking to vacate the land for a new development to be undertaken by them.

I knew I had to resolve this issue quickly and many others that followed, especially the dire financial situation of the club. Debts had piled up and suppliers were refusing to extend any more credit. Except for a one- acre land next to a mosque which the former committee had bought for RM 2.2 million with members' contributions, there were no other assets or funds available. Because of my close relationship with the then Chief Minister Datuk Abdul Ghani and other senior state officials,

we started resolving issue after issue. Thanks to the Chief Minister, we managed to get a beautiful, two-acre site next to the Johor Golf club on attractive terms from the state. Now it was time to start sourcing out funds to build a new clubhouse which was a gigantic task. Many members had left the club for good as they were not confident that a new clubhouse would be built anytime in the near future!

With the cooperation of my new committee members especially my Vice President Yai, we managed to sell the two- acre land the club owned at the same original purchase price of RM

With Dato R.S. Kumar and Dato Dr.Noorul Ameen, the Founder and architect behind the Qualitas Medical Group.

2.2 million though it was a recession time. The funds were kept in safe deposits. We also held several other functions to raise funds to settle our debts and keep the club going. In the interim, thanks to our late Highness Sultan Iskander of Johor the proposed development on our club land by the City council was shelved with his objection thus allowing us to remain there till the construction of our new clubhouse began in 2010.

It was estimated that we needed about Rm 6.5 million to build a new clubhouse and for renovation but we only had 2.2 million. Never wanting to give up, we planned and raised nearly Rm one million through a major dinner function. I helped to raise

nearly Rm 300,000. Thanks to my close relationship with the then Deputy Prime Minister Tan sri Muhiyudin we received a federal government grant of one million Ringgit. Armed with around four million Ringgit, we launched the construction of the new clubhouse in 2010 with the hope that we would be able to raise the balance money during the next two years of the construction period.

My prayers were answered when my old and close friend Dato Khaled Nordin became Chief Minister of Johor after the 2013 general elections, just in time to be invited as my chief guest to open the newly completed clubhouse on October 5th 2013. With the support of another close friend of mine Tan Sri Sharir, the Member of Parliament for Johor Bahru who had also been the political mentor for Dato Khaled Nordin, I managed to convince him to announce a state government grant of One Million Ringgit for our new clubhouse which we received promptly soon after the opening. The opening of the new clubhouse was a dream come true for many members especially the senior members who never believed that this dream would ever come true!! Thanks to all the above kind souls, a dream came true after 12 years of patience and efforts.

I would be failing in my duty if I did not recognise the contribution of the good members of the club, the committee members who stood by me, the generous donors, my friends, the consultants especially Yap the architect and above all our contractor Balamurugan of AMD Construction

The award of Tun Sambanthan was bestowed on me by the Perak Tamilar Thirunaal Organisers in January 2023

Sdn Bhd who completed the project despite a substantial sum owing to him during the final stages of construction and to Guna of Aero café who spent nearly Rm 850, 000 for renovation and refurbishment of the club as part of the agreement to manage the new club before the opening ceremony. They were God sent to us. Despite all the payments being made we still had a substantial sum owing to our contractor and suppliers. Thanks to the kind generosity of my friend and Chief Minister Datuk Khaled Nordin, we received a further grant of Rm 500,000 from him at our club's annual dinner held in January 2016 and again in May 2017 in which he was the chief guest. This helped to settle a substantial portion of the club's debts.

The successful completion of the new clubhouse had been a mammoth task and a long journey with nothing to gain financially for me except personal self- satisfaction on a job well done.

I stepped down as President of the club after fourteen years at our AGM in April 2016 paving the way for my Vice President and close friend of many years Prasad Achuthan and a new committee to take over.

Apart from my involvement in completing the new temple and club house, I had also spent considerable time on my own financial resources in promoting various economic vehicles that benefitted the Malaysian Indian community.

Apart from having raised more than a million ringgit in shares for Maika Holdings which was initiated by MIC but failed to deliver what it promised to the Indian community, I had also played a major role in raising substantial sums as share capital and

With the former Home Minister and then Chairman of FELCRA YB Dato Seri Zainudin Hamzah with my business associates from India.

With the then Home Minister YB Tan Sri Sheikh Radzi on our quest to get recognition for Silambam in SUKMA along with Mr. P.S. Pillai and Dato Kanagaraja

fixed deposits for three of the major Indian co-operatives in Malaysia, namely the National Land Finance co-operative society (NLFCS), Koperasi Nesa and Koperasi Belia Maju Jaya. Of all the three co-operatives, NLFCS has delivered the most for its members, followed by Koperasi Nesa, thanks to their management teams.

I have been a delegate for many years in these three co-operatives and had in fact been a Director and Vice Chairman of Koperasi Belia Maju Jaya for several years. Though Koperasi Maju Jaya started off very well, it has not delivered any substantial benefits to its members.

Having lost out on a substantial income for not being able to carry out my last 2 major housing projects in 1997, 1998 due to the Asian financial crisis. I had to turn to other businesses to supplement my reduced income.

I still had two General practice clinics going and I believe I made a wise decision in selling a majority share to the Qualitas medical group in 2000 when they made me an offer to buy. This group was initiated by Dato Dr. Noorul Ameen - a general Practitioner with foresight. The general practice in Malaysia had been a lucrative business for many years but was becoming tough due to stiff competition and introduction of new laws by the Ministry of Health especially the newly introduced Private Health care services act in 1998. I had envisaged then that the general practice in this

With Tan Sri Isa Samad former MB of Negeri Sembilan and chairman of FELDA, along with Mr. Paul Appadurai

With Tan Sri Imran, the President of Malaysian Olympic Council and the Executive Council Members of Malaysian Silambam Association.

country would become more difficult in the future unless there was consolidation and amalgamation into larger groups. Despite asking several of my senior colleagues to join the Qualitas group at that time they turned down the offer. What I have envisaged then has become true now!! Many of my colleagues have seen severe drop in their practices. There are more than 7000 general practices in the country whereas Qualitas has become the single largest General practice group in Malaysia and have extended their business to Singapore, Australia and India thanks to the foresight and business acumen of its founder Dato Dr Noorul Ameen and his core management team. In fact, Qualitas has diversified into several other health related businesses including dentistry and became the first general practice group in Malaysia to be listed on the Singapore stock exchange in 2008. They delisted from the stock exchange in 2009 and have now become a private entity. I am proud to be a part of this group and I still do consultancy work for them on some business ventures quite apart from doing part time locum in their clinics.

I went into a multilevel marketing business with a health product for the first time in 2000 having avoided it for many years to supplement my reduced income. With my wide network and involvement in several organisations over the years, it was also my desire to create several Malaysian Indian entrepreneurs with passive income through this business. I was able to succeed and make my

With YAB Tan Sri Ghani Bin Othman, the Chief Minister of Johor in 2010 to thank him for granting the 2 acres of land for our new Club House of JCSC.

mark in this multilevel business when I recruited a substantial number of Indian distributors throughout Malaysia. While I believe Multi-level business is good to be involved in for a continuous passive income especially if you have a good health product to market, it also involves hard continuous work, honesty and good team spirit.

Unfortunately, not all of the distributors in my team were able to put in enough time and work. Many got involved with a lot of enthusiasm in the beginning but subsequently dropped out. I realised this and ceased it in 2001 as I had earned a substantial income in the last two years.

My old business partner Lim Chee Hiong contacted me in 2002 and spoke to me about a new business called Voice over Internet Protocol which was sweeping across the Asean region. He asked me whether I would be able to secure a licence from the Malaysian Multimedia Commission that I readily agreed to try. Thanks to the political connection I still had and with the help of Datuk Subramaniam I was able to secure one of the first 9 licenses that was approved by the Multimedia Commission. I still remember vividly one of the other approved licence holders offering me two million Ringgit to transfer the licence to him saying it was an unfamiliar business to me knowing I was a medical practioner. Lim Chee Hiong and his partner Michael who were the initiators and major investors in our company rejected the offer saying we would be making more than that in running the business. As planned and envisaged by Lim Chee Hion, the business took off very well and became a multimillion ringgit business in the next two years. Though I was holding 40% shares in the company and as the local director received a monthly income. I was unfamiliar with the technical aspects of the business and was only involved in administration and securing clients for our business.

While the turnover of our company was in millions, our margin of profits was thin because of the stiff competition from our competitors who were numerous by now. Despite the competition, our service was quite popular in the market. We were quite comfortable, when out of the blues problems

cropped up between Lim and Michael, my major shareholders who had been childhood friends. This led to their decision in wanting to part ways and to cease business in Malaysia in 2006. Though they handed over the company to me after having cleared all the outstanding issues, my efforts to source new shareholders familiar with this business failed and neither could I find outright buyers to purchase the company as there were already more than 250 VOIP licences that had been issued by the Multimedia Commission!!

It shocked me that a childhood relationship could crumble to nothing and completely destroy a potential and viable multi-million- dollar business!

I continued working as a consultant on several projects for different companies. One of them was Edisijuta Parking Sdn Bhd, owned by Indran who introduced the first private parking concept and business in 2001 in Sri Lanka. Indran, who was well versed in the parking business had acted as a consultant for his friend Deo, who was the major shareholder in our car -parking venture in Sri Lanka. Though I was not close to Indran during that point of time, it turned out to be one of the best things I had done in my life. I had the opportunity to work with him on two projects for which he rewarded me handsomely. I have never seen a more honest, dedicated, upright and knowledgeable person like him. Though he is younger to me, he never fails to put his thoughts and views strongly and clearly as he is knowledgeable in many fields!! He is one

With my friend and benefactor YAB Tan Sri Muhiyuddin in 2020 on his appointment as 8th Prime Minister of Malaysia.

of the finest human beings I have met in my life. A man of honour and truth! I am still working with him on certain projects and hope to succeed further!!

One of the many organisations that I worked and cared for is the Malaysian Medical Association. Though I had represented the Johor MMA committee as their Private Practice Section (PPS) representative at the national level in 2001, I could not play an active role in MMA till 2013 when I was elected as the Chairman of the PPS section

The New JCSC Club House

of MMA. My election at the AGM in 2013 was a last minute and sudden decision initiated by Datuk Dr. Pandu, a family friend of mine from Malacca. While driving down together from Kuala Lumpur to Nilai in Negeri Sembilan where our MMA AGM was being held, out of the blues he suggested I should contest as Chairman of PPS since I have been an active vociferous speaker in most of the AGMs. I was reluctant at first, but he managed to convince me to contest and within an hour of campaign before the PPS AGM. I was elected as the new PPS Chairman defeating the incumbent Dr. Koh Kar Chai to the surprise of many!

As usual I started working with enthusiasm and commitment with my new team. I believe we attained two major successes during our two-year term when we were able to secure a new and equitable consultancy fees after 14 long years of negotiation for the GPs from Perkeso or Socso, a government agency that pays for the medical benefits of injured employees. The second success I believe was when for the first time in the history of MMA we managed to raise a clean profit of RM 100,000 from a very successful GP seminar held under my leadership. Though I would attribute both these successes to the support given by the MMA members and my PPS team, I was able to contribute substantially as I had the political and social connections.

Having served for two years as PPS chairman I contested for one of the two Deputy Secretaries posts in MMA in 2015 and won with the highest

votes in a four -cornered contest. During the next one year as Deputy secretary, I was able to revamp the entire tendering exercise in MMA. I helped in introducing a new insurance company JLT through my friend, Mr. Len to MMA to provide indemnity to our members with better incentives and income to both our members and MMA. I had also helped to successfully raise more than Rm 120,000 from sponsors for the various states that had organised our National MMA Annual General meetings from 2014 to 2016.

Having contributed substantially to MMA, I contested for the President Elect post of MMA in 2016 hoping to provide a strong and farsighted leadership. I lost this time against the incumbent General Secretary Nevertheless, despite the defeat, I recontested for the same post again in 2018 and won paving the way for me to serve MMA again as the President.

I am proud that as President elect from 2018 to 2019 and subsequently as President from 2019 to 2020, I had seen several successes which I attribute to the strong support I received from my members and to the dedicated and hard working staff of MMA under the leadership of the Chief Operating Officer of MMA, Mrs.Rissa.

During my two years as President Elect and President of MMA, we managed to raise nearly RM 1 million in funds from our various activities namely the National MMA AGM of MMA in 2019 where I was installed as President and from the First ever Nationwide Health Carnival Event held on 18th January 2020. In total during my six years stint in MMA as office bearer in various positions, I had helped to raise a total of Rm 1.4 Million.

I am also proud to note that for the first time ever during my term as President I had arranged to meet more than nine cabinet Ministers including the 8th Prime Minister, Tan Sri Muhiyuddin Yassin and the present 10th Prime Minister Datuk Seri Anwar Ibrahim to better explain the role played by MMA in the Healthcare sector of the country and the various issues faced by our members both in the government and private sectors.

After the change of government in February 2020, we were able to meet with the Minister Of Health Datuk Seri Dr.Adham Baba and his Deputy Datuk Dr.Noor Azmi, both of whom were General Practitioners before assuming their government posts.

The calamity and destruction of the Covid 19 infection and the fight against it brought new norms to all our lives including MMA. To battle the scourge and to support our front liners,under my initiative, we in MMA, launched the COVID FUND together with our tax exempt MMA Foundation and SHOPPEE, the on line shopping platform. Thanks to the generous public and to Tan Sri R.Doraisingam our current President of MMA Foundation and his friends, we were able to raise a respectable RM 1 Million within 3 months and the funds have been distributed to the various states and Frontliners in need of these funds.

I stepped down as the President of MMA in September 2020 to become the Immediate Past President,having served historically for 16 months despite my tenure being only for one year, all due to the Covid infection!!

I am a sort of COVID 19 President!!

Despite these critical times, I managed to celebrate my 70th birthday in August 2020 this year amongst my family,relatives and close friends to get away from the thoughts of this dreaded Covid.

At present, I have limited my involvement in public life after almost 40 years of active participation in various organisations. I hope to develope the Johor Indian Education Fund(which is being renamed the Malaysian Indian Education Fund)and which was established in 2000 by my friends and supporters on my 50th birthday into a strong entity in the next few years.

I believe I have contributed with honesty, dedication and with a certain amount of success in every organisation that I had led and have been involved in. I sincerely hope and pray that all those who have taken over these organisations will continue the good work with the same dedication, honesty and determination.

I am still working as a consultant on few projects especially with Indran and with Len both of whom I consider as my good and sincere friends of many years. I believe both of them will always be there for me when I need their help and advice.

My journey till now has been a long and ardous one with many valuable lessons learnt whether success or failure. Many have contributed to my well being and understanding of people in the long journey of my life and I would be failing in my duty if I do not acknowledge all them.

With YB Liow Tiong Lai the then
Deputy minister of Sports and
Mr. P.S. Pillai, Vice President of
Malaysian Silambam Association

As President of Malaysian Silambam Association
from 2002 - 2008. Photos taken at National Silambam
Competition in Sabah.

At the wedding receptions of my Eldest
daughter Dr. Ashwini with Ganesh Sayapathy
in Kuala Lumpur and in Johor Bharu in 2007

My Days in MMA

As the MMA PPS Chairman from 2013 to 2015 as the Deputy Secretary 2015-2016 and as President Elect, President and Immediate Past President from 2018-2021.

The following were the achivements during my period in MMA:

- Raising RM1.5 million for MMA
- Getting SOCSO panel clinic fees revised after 14 years.
- Conducting the first nationwide MMA Health Carnival
- Initiating a Covid Fund and raising RM1 million with the support of Shopee and MMA Foundation
- As the President of MMA i have attended several International Medical Confrences and i have served as the Vice President of Commenwealth Medical Association.
- We have met more than 9 Cabinet Ministers and other important government officials during my Presidentship to explain the role and importance of MMA in the Health sector.

With the CEO of MMA Ms. Rissa and the dedicated staff of MMA in 2020 as the President of MMA

My days in MMA between 2019 and 2020 as President.

The MoU Signing Ceremony
between

Launch of the first National Health Carnival in MMA on January 2020. Special Guests included Dr. Agarwal, the President of CMAAO, the then Health Minister YB Datuk Zulkifly and Past Presidents of MMA. A grant of RM200,000 was given by YB Lim Guan Eng as Finance Minister. A total amount of nearly RM850,000 was raised in cash and benefits.

Launch of Shopee, MMA Foundation and MMA Covid-19 Fund in 2020.
An amount of RM 1 million was raised for various activities.

My 50th Birthday Celebration in 2000 organised in Johor Baru by my well wishers. Was well attended by several friends from all over Malaysia. The Johor Indian Education Fund was launched and a sum of RM50,000 was collected to mark my birthday occassion.

I am deeply honoured to have met and known
six Prime Ministers of Malaysia.

Tengku Abdul Rahman

Tun Dr. Mahathir

Tun Abdullah Ahmad Badawi

Tan Sri Muhyiddin Yassin

Dato' Sri Ismail Sabri Yaakob

Datuk Seri Anwar Ibrahim

C. N. Annadurai

M.G.Ramachandran

J.Jayalalitha

M.K.Stalin

Kalaignar M.Karunanidhi

Actor Prabhu

Kavingar Vairamuthu

**With Indian Film personalities
and other prominent citizens**

Seergazhi Dr. Sivasithambaram

Actress Revathy

Actor Jaishankar

Actor S.S. Rajendran

Minister Doraimurugan

With Late Tan Sri Subrmaniam, Assembly Speaker Thamizhkudimagan, and Minister Veerasamy

The Johor Education Fund which was founded in 2000 has collected more than RM500,000 and has disbursed several loans to needy students and has supported several educational seminars in Primary Tamil and secondary schools. This organisation has been well supported by dedicated friends, kind donors and committee members.

At my 70th Birthday Celebration in Kuala Lumpur
and Johor Bharu

Madras Blues Night organised in 2017 for a gathering of Madras Graduates and their friends. Raised an amount of RM20,000 and donated to charitable organisations.

'Aadiya Aatam Aadiyil'

A gathering of friends and supporters of Tan Sri S.Subramaniam, Datuk K.Padmanathan and Tan Sri M.G. Pandithan was held in July 2022. More than 180 friends from all over Malaysia attended the above function.

To commemorate the function a sum of RM30,000 was collected from various kind donors and contributed to Dr. Rama Subbiah Scholarship Fund.

Acknowledging a Journey Enriched by Hearts and Hands

- My gratitude to the almighty for having blessed me with wonderful grandparents and loving parents.

- To my loving wife and my 3 children for having played a great part in my life journey.

- To my dearest siblings and their families for the love and respect they have shown me.

- To my brother-in-law Jambulingam who always had a place in my heart.

- To all my dedicated teachers who have made me for what I am today.

- To all my dear friends, colleagues and donors who had stood with me in the various Organisations that I had headed and had been part of and for giving their support in the success of the various public and private projects that I had undertaken.

- My school, college and university classmates especially Raghbir Singh, Dato Donald Choo , Dato Choo Keng Weng and Bobby Chin who stood with me throughout my life.

- To the friends and colleagues of my late father especially Mr.R.Balakrishnan, Mr.R. Kathiravelu, Mr Anandan and Mr. P.Govindasamy who stood with him during his difficult times and last days.

- To Mr.Lim Chee Hiong of ATD (S) Pte Ltd.

- Tan Sri K.R.Somasundaram, Chairman of NLFCS

- Datuk P.Sahadevan, Managing Director of NLFCS.

- Late Mr Vadivelu, Former Treasurer of NLFCS

- Late Mr Srimalan, Former GM of NLFCS.

- Mr .G.Indran and Ms Grace of Edisijuta Parking Sdn Bhd

- Mr. Len M.S.of Inmaco Sdn BHD

- Who stood and supported me in all of my business and financial dealings.

To my political Mentors

- Tan Sri S Subramaniam, the former Deputy President of MIC and Deputy Minister

- and Datuk.K.Patmanaban, the former Vice President of MIC and Deputy Minister

My political friends and colleagues both in MIC and IPF especially

- Tan Sri M.G.Pandithan, Former Vice President of MIC and President of IPF

- Tan Sri. K.Kumaran, Former Vice Presdent of MIC and Deputy Minister

- Tan Sri G.Raju, Former Chairman of MIC Perak and Perak EXCO Member

- Datuk V.L.Kandan, Former Youth Leader of MIC and Selangor EXCO Member

To all my political friends from other political parties,

- Tan Sri Sharir Abdul Samad, Former MP of Johor Bahru and Minister
- Tan Sri.Muhiyuddin Yassin, former MB of Johor and former Prime Minister
- Tan Sri Ghani Osman, Former MB of Johor and former Minister
- Datuk Seri Ismail Saberi, Former Minister of Sports and former Prime Minister
- Datuk Seri Khalid Nordin, former Menteri Besar of Johor and current Minister of Higher Education
- Tan Sri Rais Yatim, Former Minister and President of Senate

for their kindness and support in making all my public and private projects a success.

- To our current Prime Minister Datuk Seri Anwar Ibrahim who has been a friend for many years and who was kind enough to offer me a position in politics in 2013 which I had to kindly decline.

To my personal family friends

- The late Mr. Athikumanan, Editor, Malaysia Nanban)
- Tan Sri R.Doraisingam, Datuk R.Ramalingam, Datuk R. Naga Sundaram, Ms.R.Indira (Lotus group of Companies) and their families for their continous love and support for my family and siblings

- Mr.OMS Thiagarajan, Klang for his continous support.
- Mr Munusamy (PAKA)
- Mr.M.Elango (Masai)
- Mr.Sashi Raman velu.
- Tan Sri S.Selva
- AMD Mr. Bala and
- Aerocafe Mr.Guna for their continous support to our family and siblings
- To the family of Late J.Sarangapany of Singapore, Maran, Viji their siblings and families for their love and support.
- To all the medical and Health personnel especially Dr.Edmond Ong, Prof Dr.Sharul, Prof. Dr.V.Nathan and Dr.Raghu Varadaraju who took extreme care of me during my serious illness and hospitalisation in 2021.
- To the many contributors who helped me to recover from my illness in 2021 especially Tan Sri Doraisingam, Dato Prakadesh Kumar, Sarojini Ruth, Segaran Mathavan, Dato Seri Raj, Dato Muthukumar, Dato Seri Krishnamoorthy my other various friends and colleagues..
- To all my media friends who have stood with me since my entry into Political and Public Life since 1976.
- To all those who I have inadvertently left out to thank them with gratitude.

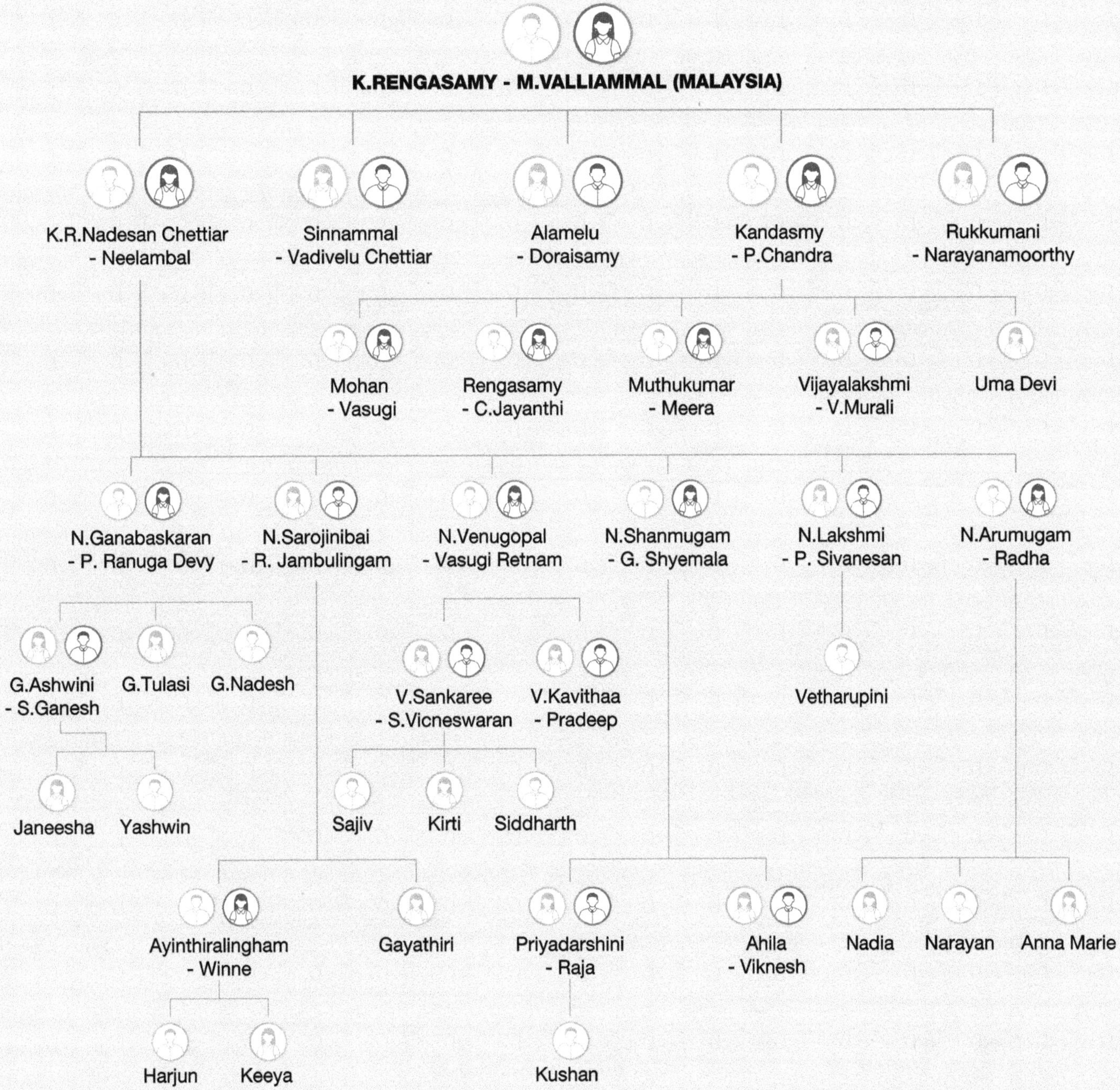

K.RENGASAMY - M.VALLIAMMAL (MALAYSIA)

K.R.Nadesan Chettiar - Neelambal
Sinnammal - Vadivelu Chettiar
Alamelu - Doraisamy
Kandasmy - P.Chandra
Rukkumani - Narayanamoorthy

Mohan - Vasugi
Rengasamy - C.Jayanthi
Muthukumar - Meera
Vijayalakshmi - V.Murali
Uma Devi

N.Ganabaskaran - P. Ranuga Devy
N.Sarojinibai - R. Jambulingam
N.Venugopal - Vasugi Retnam
N.Shanmugam - G. Shyemala
N.Lakshmi - P. Sivanesan
N.Arumugam - Radha

G.Ashwini - S.Ganesh
G.Tulasi
G.Nadesh
V.Sankaree - S.Vicneswaran
V.Kavithaa - Pradeep
Vetharupini

Janeesha
Yashwin
Sajiv
Kirti
Siddharth

Ayinthiralingham - Winne
Gayathiri
Priyadarshini - Raja
Ahila - Viknesh
Nadia
Narayan
Anna Marie

Harjun
Keeya
Kushan

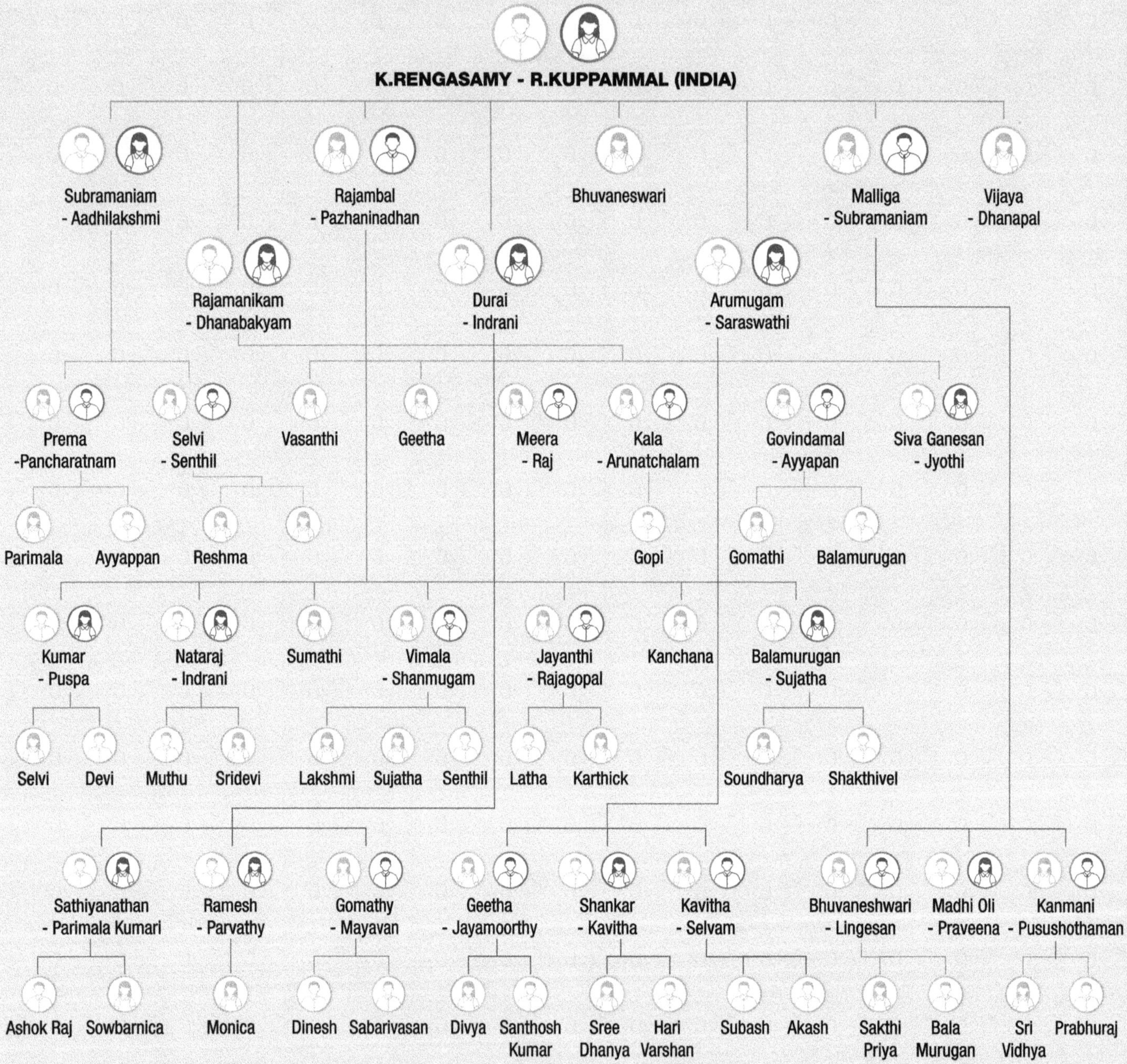

K.RENGASAMY - R.KUPPAMMAL (INDIA)

Subramaniam - Aadhilakshmi
Rajambal - Pazhaninadhan
Bhuvaneswari
Malliga - Subramaniam
Vijaya - Dhanapal

Rajamanikam - Dhanabakyam
Durai - Indrani
Arumugam - Saraswathi

Prema - Pancharatnam
Selvi - Senthil
Vasanthi
Geetha
Meera - Raj
Kala - Arunatchalam
Govindamal - Ayyapan
Siva Ganesan - Jyothi

Parimala
Ayyappan
Reshma
Gopi
Gomathi
Balamurugan

Kumar - Puspa
Nataraj - Indrani
Sumathi
Vimala - Shanmugam
Jayanthi - Rajagopal
Kanchana
Balamurugan - Sujatha

Selvi
Devi
Muthu
Sridevi
Lakshmi
Sujatha
Senthil
Latha
Karthick
Soundharya
Shakthivel

Sathiyanathan - Parimala Kumari
Ramesh - Parvathy
Gomathy - Mayavan
Geetha - Jayamoorthy
Shankar - Kavitha
Kavitha - Selvam
Bhuvaneshwari - Lingesan
Madhi Oli - Praveena
Kanmani - Pusushothaman

Ashok Raj
Sowbarnica
Monica
Dinesh
Sabarivasan
Divya
Santhosh Kumar
Sree Dhanya
Hari Varshan
Subash
Akash
Sakthi Priya
Bala Murugan
Sri Vidhya
Prabhuraj

To my dear children and the future generations

Surfing through my trials and tribulations in the last 45 years I wish to pen all that helped me to have the drive to reach for the stars for my children and the future generation.

1. Thank God for all the good things given to you in your life. Believe in him and yourself when the going gets tough.

2. Love and respect your parents and never forget you owe them everything for what you are today.

3. Be charitable in your life and give back to society whatever you may be able to give even if it is small.

4. Always be grateful to all those who have helped you in any way in your life.

5. Treat all human beings alike whether they are from the highest or lowest strata of society.

6. Learn to forgive all those who have hurt you in anyway.

7. Never say die, give your best and maximum effort to succeed in whatever you aspire to do.

8. Be humble in life.

9. Listen to your conscience and always do what is right in life.

10. Plan your future well for both you and your family

God Bless You

- Dr Ganabaskaran Nadesan

My journey with Dr. Baskaran set sail 20 over years ago. We were business associates traveling to India and Sri Lanka in search of financial success.

It bloomed into something much more that and has lasted through the years. Dr. became a father like figure and a good friend and we have been fortunate to have cross roads in our lives.

He is a good man filled with a passion to serve others, at the expense of his own well-being. This has led him on a roller coaster life but with loads of friends and people who have benefitted from his generosity. I believe that if Dr. had a chance to relive his life, he would still put the interest of others, in front of his. I continue to wish him good health and happiness, as he continues his life journey.

- Indran Gnanamoorthy

I have known Dr Baskaran for many years and he is a true and sincere person who is ever ready to offer his presence and helps in good or bad time. He is also one of the most principled politicians who has unwavered loyalty with the genuine and noble mission to serve. I am privileged to have him as a GOOD buddy and will always cherish our everlasting friendship

- Len Min Sin

It was a privilege and honour to have known the late Mr. Nadeson Chettiar a staunch supporter and family friend of my late brother Tan Sri V Manickavasagam. He was a well-known philanthropist and famous for his lavish "virunthombal" (hospitality par excellence) – Man of great integrity, trustworthiness and helpful at all times.

His son Datuk Dr Ganabaskaran took after his father like duck to water and continued with his father's political and social contributions, as early as in his student days in Medical School in India.

It is a great pity and loss to the community that Dr Ganabaskaran amongst others was sidelined from public service after Tan Sri Manicka passed on.

- Datuk V.L. Kandan

A rollercoaster journey of 72 years with its joys and tears successes and failures, wealth and its loss, friends and foes, he had it all, he had seen it all. Dr Ganabaskaran, with unwavering faith in Almighty, manoeuvred through tough times in his life, and is now sharing his story with relatives and friends. A comprehensive and historical recall of events over three generations, with a deeper insight into his own life, he has made it an interesting and easy read for all. For a person who is forever busy and travelling, I can see his great passion and effort in the content of this book and I congratulate Dr Ganabaskaran and wish him well.

- Major General Dato Pahlawan Dr R. Mohanadas (Rtd)

Dr ganabaskaran whom I know since 1978 is a very dynamic and team oriented leader. Very focused in whatever he does and is result oriented.

- S. Sivaraj

A powerful narration of his life experiences every young person has to read to understand the struggles of a Malaysian more so a Malaysian of Indian origin. I have known him for about 20 years. A Medical Doctor who was always in the forefront in making sure that the community is taken care of. He was a man committed to whatever he takes on as his responsibility. For instance, he was the President of the Malaysian Medical Association during the Pandemic and his work was exemplary during the period in making sure that the medical fraternity got whatever was needed in addressing the issues that appeared. He was there for anyone who needed his services all the time. He had a brief illustrious political career which he presents in this book which can be a great lesson for anyone aspiring to become a politician especially in a race based political party. In sum the incidents in this narration are absorbing and laden with messages that Malaysians need to ponder. His experiences are shared with freshness, intensity and power. Datuk Dr Baskaran is a successful medical professional, a great and wise friend and above all a family man who has succeeded in creating a family of committed professionals.

- Professor Nathan Vytialingam
Honorary Fellow World Federation of Occupational Therapist

Dear Reader,

Having been friends for over 50 years, I am thrilled to introduce you to this captivating story told by Datuk Dr. Ganabaskaran (Baskaran). This book takes us on a heartfelt journey through three generations of his family, tracing back to his immigrant grandfather, Rengasamy Chettiar, who established a thriving business empire in JB through pure hard work. Baskaran and I have shared numerous adventures, starting from our cherished school days as classmates, and our families' paths have intersected in ways that make this story all the more special. The pages of this book bring back vivid memories, especially of our secondary school years at English College JB, where I discovered Baskaran's outgoing nature and remarkable talents in academics, sports, and music. Who could forget the Tamil version of "Tom Dooley" by the Kingston Trio, which Baskaran performed with his band the Microwave 5? As I read about his life, I am also reminded of the Diwali celebrations at Baskaran's home, where we sensed the deep respect and reverence he had for his father. From there, his journey unfolds with fearlessness, excelling in medical school, establishing a thriving medical practice, and embracing a path in politics, echoing his father's legacy. Now, I offer a warm invitation for you to immerse yourself in this wonderful, uninhibited account of his family's journey. I have no doubt that you will find joy, humor, and inspiration in these pages, just as I did.

- Raghbir Dhillon
EC Class of 1967

Nowadays, not many modern parents of diaspora communities will have the time nor inclination to narrate the story or history of the journeys of their forebears to the new lands where they now reside. To be sure, these sojourners in charting a new course for their progenies that are to follow would have faced immense challenges to survive in their new surroundings. Every sojourner and their ensuing generations would have interesting stories to tell.. and often they become compelling lessons for succeeding generations on survival itself. Baskaran in narrating the stories of his grandfather, his father and himself did a yeoman's duty to his progenies and future generations in this regard. It is also an example to all parents that this is what they need to do. Did not Laotze, one of the most illustrious and probably the wisest of the ancient Chinese sages write in some verses of the Tao Te Ching:

Just realise where you came from...
'This is the essence of wisdom'.

- Chin See Wah

My dear Baskaran,

It gives me great pleasure to be able to write a few words about our long lasting friendship. Needless to say, our sweet memories goes back to our English College days where we had the best learning experience in our lives. I still remember the good times when I used to come to your house to play and enjoyed your kind wonderful mum's delicious curry. Amongst our classmates, i think both of us were the more adventurous and naughty ones than the rest. Words cannot describe how wonderful those days were growing up with you as a good friend.

We have finally reached this age and to be blessed that we can still meet occasionally. I must congratulate you for doing so well in your career as a Doctor, a Politician and as a Businessman. I remember how you went through your difficult times bringing your children through University and am glad are all doing well today. Also you have a wonderful and successful wife who supports whatever you do. I treasure to have you as a long and true friend and I hope this will continue for many years to come.

Dato Choo Keng Kit.

Congratulations to Dato Dr. N.G. Baskaran on the completion of your book, showcasing your unwavering perseverance and determination. This remarkable addition to the literary landscape will undoubtedly contribute to the rich tapestry of works chronicling the development of our beloved nation, Malaysia. When I think of my friend and fellow alumnus from English College Johor Bahru, several words come to mind: gregarious, fun-loving, helpful, and loyal. Our time together was filled with shared study sessions, memorable dramatic performances, spirited debates, and joyous singing sessions. These experiences created a treasure trove of cherished memories for all of us.

Although it has been more than 56 years since we last roamed the playing fields of EC, we have kept us physically apart, we have managed to maintain a meaningful connection. I commend you on your successful career, your lovingly nurtured family, the encompassing journey you have embarked on, including your years in politics, your dedicated service to the community, and your numerous leadership roles.

Your book masterfully captures the trials and tribulations endured by your grandparents and parents, ultimately culminating in the person you have become today. It is a testament to their legacy and the indomitable spirit that resides within you. May you continue this remarkable journey, my friend, enriching the lives of those you encounter along the way.

Dato Ir. Ibrahim Abu Bakar

Awarded the Datukship Panglima
Mahkota Wilayah (PMW) in 2021
by Duli Yang Maha Mulia Seri
Paduka Baginda Yang di-Pertuan
Agong in recognition of my public
service in various organisations.